The Cooking W

15 Minute Cookbook:

100 "no-stress" tasty vegan recipes that anyone can cook in 15 minutes or less!

www.CookingWithPlants.com

The Cooking With Plants 15 Minute Cookbook: 100 "no-stress" easy vegan recipes that anyone can cook in 15 minutes or less!
© 2018 Anja Cass. All rights reserved.

Business Contact: admin@cookingwithplants.com
Website: www.cookingwithplants.com

ISBN: 978-1-925833-20-1 (paperback)
         978-1-925833-21-8 (eBook)

The Cataloguing-in-Publication entry can be viewed at the National Library of Australia. Reference NLApp78137

CONTENTS

AUTHOR BIO - MEET ANJA

Anja Cass was born in Germany in 1973. At the age of eight she moved to Australia with her parents and soon discovered the joys of different cultures and foods.

It wasn't until she went to University to study a Bachelor of Communications, that she moved away from home and had to cook for herself. Living on campus with many overseas students, she was further exposed to ingredients and cooking techniques from all around the globe.

Anja's passion for food and cooking grew over the next twenty years as she continued to cook for family and friends on a daily basis.

However, in 2012 a health scare struck. After a routine doctor's appointment it was found that she had a bulging aorta and the onset of heart disease. With a young son and family history of fatal heart disease on both sides of her family, she researched ways to reverse this. Everything led to a *Plant Based Diet*.

She began cooking plant based food and saw immediate results. Her cholesterol dropped, she had energy again, and she lost 24 kilos (over 50 pounds) in just five months.

Anja's weight loss and healthy glow had people questioning what she was eating. So in 2013 she started to do quick YouTube videos to explain and show her new meals to family and friends.

What happened next was never expected...

More and more people started to watch her channel - strangers!

People from all around the world were tuning in for her quick, easy and tasty recipes. Behold - Cooking With Plants!

Following on from this, Anja authored a range of best selling cookbooks, delivering courses and won the 2015 Vegan of the Year Award for Social Media Outreach.

She is a popular and well-loved vegan cook who inspires her followers to eat well and get healthy with whole plants based recipes. Her tagline "Vegan Made Easy" says it all. She really does keep things quick and easy with recipes that taste amazing.

A WORD FROM ANJA

I know what it's like to be busy, especially during the week. When it comes to weekday cooking, you want something fast, easy and tasty. Better still, if it can actually be good for you... then high five to that!

So that's exactly why I created this cookbook. 100 "no-stress" tasty vegan recipes that anyone can cook in 15 minutes or less!

If you do not yet know my background, I lost over 50 pounds (24 kilos) after heart-health issues led me to a plant based lifestyle in 2012. Since then I have easily maintained my weight and improved my health and vitality.

Be sure to follow me on social media and join the free recipe newsletter on my website for all of my latest plant based delights!

- www.cookingwithplants.com
- cookingwithplants
- cookingwithplants
- @cookingwithplants
- cookingwithplants/vegan-recipes

I hope you enjoy these recipes as much as I have enjoyed creating them for you!

COMMON SUBSTITUTIONS:

If you have an allergy or don't like certain ingredients, it is very easy to substitute with something else when using most of my recipes.

Here is a quick list of ideas to help you think outside the box and use the ingredients that you have on hand.

Nuts: for example, instead of cashews or other nuts, use sunflower seeds, chickpeas/garbanzo beans, cannellini beans, cooked cauliflower or corn kernels.

Mushrooms: if you don't like mushrooms, think of the texture they provide. Use things such as eggplant, chunky zucchini or cauliflower in their place.

Eggplant: if you don't like eggplant, think of the texture it provides. Use things such as mushrooms, chunky zucchini or cauliflower in its place.

Miso Paste: If you do not have miso paste on hand you can use a mixture of tahini (sesame paste) mixed with a bit of soy sauce. If you are avoiding miso because of the soy content, then you can always get miso made from rice or chickpeas instead. You could also use a salted mushroom paste. Just cook some mushrooms and blend them with a little bit of coarse celtic sea salt or a touch of soy sauce to get that same umami flavor.

Soy/Tofu: If you are allergic or do not want to use soy products, just opt for alternatives. For example, instead of soy sauce, use coconut aminos. Instead of soy milk use almond, rice, coconut, hemp or any other alternate plant based milk. Instead of tofu use other beans such as cannellini beans or chickpeas/garbanzo beans. If you are avoiding beans altogether, quite often you can use potato or cauliflower in its place.

Oil: If, like me, you don't use oil in your cooking or are wanting to remove it from your cooking, then here are some options for you. Instead of frying in oil, get yourself a good quality non-stick pan and just use a splash of water or vegetable broth just like you would oil. In actual recipes such as those for baking, use things such as apple sauce, mashed banana, mashed sweet potato, psyllium husks, chia seeds or flax meal mixed with some water. In other recipes you might be able to use tahini, peanut butter, almond butter, plant based milk or even coconut water. I have even found that using the brine from canned chickpeas or other beans actually also works really well - even for things such as baked potatoes.

WHAT IF I'M MISSING AN INGREDIENT OR DON'T LIKE SOMETHING?

All of the recipes in this book are very forgiving and are essentially a guide of what you can make for a quick meal. If you don't have some of the ingredients asked for in a recipe, try to think of something similar that you could use. For example, if you don't have vegetable stock, use water and a pinch of salt, or water and a dash of soy sauce.

Also if you don't like mushrooms, think of something that has a similar texture or consistency, as well as a similar type of flavor that you could use instead. For example, courgettes/zucchini and a dash of soy sauce would give a similar texture and flavor to the same recipe.

If you don't have fresh herbs, use dried.

If you don't like your food too salty, leave the salt out, or add other spices and condiments that you prefer.

The recipes that call for nutritional yeast flakes can usually have this as an optional ingredient. Otherwise, you could also use a touch of tahini mixed with some soy sauce or a bit of miso paste to mimic a similar flavor.

ARE YOUR MEASUREMENTS METRIC OR IMPERIAL?

In this cookbook I actually give the measurements for both.

When I create recipes I usually use metric measurements, however unless you are baking bread or a cake, they are close enough to the imperial amounts to really not make any difference to the taste and final result of the dish.

The recipes that I make are extremely forgiving and I often measure very roughly when I first develop recipes. In most cases it really don't matter if you leave something out or don't quite have enough of something or too much of another thing.

The main difference is that a metric cup is 250ml and an imperial cup is 240ml. It's really not a big difference.

Also, both measurements are the same for a teaspoon - 5ml.

A tablespoon in metric is 20ml and imperial is 15ml. So this can make a slight difference in rare cases... but not in this book. Happy cooking!

One Pot Wonders

Cream of Broccoli Soup pg.15

Chickpea Spinach Almond Butter Curry pg. 17

Super Quick "Cheesy" Mac Pasta pg.30

CREAM OF CORN SOUP

Serves: 1 without sides | 2 with sides

Suggested Sides: crusty bread, rice, quinoa

INGREDIENTS

275g/10oz corn kernels (fresh, canned or frozen)

2 cups/500ml unsweetened plant milk (eg. soy, almond, rice etc)

3 tsp cornstarch (cornflour)

1 tsp dried onion flakes

¼ tsp coarse celtic sea salt (or to taste)

⅛ tsp white pepper

2 tbsp nutritional yeast flakes, optional

Dash nutmeg or paprika

INSTRUCTIONS

1 Place all of the ingredients in a pot, do not put on heat yet. Stir everything together and mix well so that the flour is mixed through properly and there are no lumps.

2 Now put pot on medium to high heat and stir so that the mixture heats and thickens evenly.

3 Stir for about 5 to 10 minutes until it thickens to your liking.

4 Serve sprinkled with a dash of nutmeg or paprika!

5 Great served with a side of crusty bread... YUM!

KALE & WHITE BEAN TOMATO SOUP

Serves: 2 without sides | 4 with sides

Suggested Sides: crusty bread, rice, quinoa

INSTRUCTIONS

1 Place all of the ingredients into a pot and bring to a boil, then lower the heat and simmer for 5 minutes!

INGREDIENTS

2 cups finely chopped kale leaves (keep stalks for juicing)

400g/14oz can diced tomatoes

400g/14oz can white beans (eg. cannellini, white beans or any beans of choice), drained

1 tsp smoked paprika

1 tsp dried onion flakes

1 tsp coarse celtic sea salt (or to taste)

⅛ tsp white pepper

1 tbsp dried mixed Italian herbs

ITALIAN STYLE POTATO ZUCCHINI SOUP

Serves: 4 without sides | 8 with sides

Suggested Sides: crusty bread, rice, quinoa

INGREDIENTS

570g/20oz potatoes, sliced thinly

2 litres/quarts water

1 large zucchini, diced into small pieces

1 tsp smoked paprika

1 tsp dried onion flakes

1 tsp garlic powder

1 tsp coarse celtic sea salt (or to taste)

¼ tsp white pepper

1 tbsp dried mixed Italian herbs

5-10 olives, sliced

INSTRUCTIONS

1 Bring the water to a boil in a large pot covered with a lid. While this is happening, slice the potatoes and add them to the pot as soon as you can. Leave lid on and let them boil.

2 Chop the zucchini and add to the pot as soon as possible. Again, replace the lid and leave to boil.

3 Add all of the other ingredients and let boil with the lid of for another 10 minutes until the potatoes are soft.

 RECIPE NOTES

Add a jar of salsa and a tin of your favorite beans for an extra added depth of flavor in just seconds!

CREAM OF BROCCOLI SOUP

Serves: 1 without sides | 2 with sides

Suggested Sides: crusty bread

INGREDIENTS

250g/9oz broccoli florets, cut into thumb sized pieces

2 cups/500ml plant milk, unsweetened eg. soy, almond, coconut

3 tsp cornstarch (cornflour)

1 tsp dried onion flakes

1 tsp garlic powder

½ tsp coarse celtic sea salt (or to taste)

⅛ tsp white pepper

2 tbsp nutritional yeast flakes, optional

Freshly cracked pepper for serving

INSTRUCTIONS

1 Place all of the ingredients in a pot, not on heat yet. Stir everything together and mix well so that the flour is mixed through properly and there are no lumps.

2 Now put pot on medium to high heat and stir so that the mixture heats and thickens evenly. Stir for about 5 to 10 minutes until it thickens to your liking.

3 Serve topped with freshly cracked pepper.

 RECIPE NOTES

Do not use the broccoli stalk in this recipe as it can take a long time to soften. This is a quick meal, so keep your stalk for making a vegetable stock or for juicing. Also, if you want your soup creamier, just blend half or all of it so you don't have actual broccoli pieces in there. Enjoy!

ONION, MUSHROOM & CREAMY DIJON SOUP

Serves: 2

Suggested Sides: crusty bread

INGREDIENTS

1 onion, sliced
150g/5oz mushrooms, sliced
1 tsp minced garlic, fresh or from a jar
1 cup plant milk
1 cup boiled water
2 litres/quarts water
3 tsp cornstarch
1 tbsp Dijon mustard
1 tsp coarse celtic sea salt
3 tsp white vinegar
Black pepper, freshly cracked to serve

INSTRUCTIONS

1 Place onion, mushrooms and garlic in a small pot and cook until onion starts to brown and the mushrooms start to release their juices. Add a bit of the boiled water if it starts to stick.

2 In the meantime, mix all of the remaining ingredients (except the vinegar and pepper) in a cup and stir until the cornstarch is mixed in and there are no lumps.

3 Add the cornstarch mixture to the pot and stir everything till well combined.

4 Turn heat down to simmer and cook another 5 minutes.

 RECIPE NOTES

Serve hot and top with some freshly cracked pepper.

CHICKPEA SPINACH ALMOND BUTTER CURRY

Serves: 2 without sides | 4 with sides

Suggested Sides: rice or Naan bread

INGREDIENTS

Sauce:

1 clove garlic (or 1 tsp minced garlic in jar)

125ml/4floz (½ cup) almond butter

125ml/4floz (½ cup) soy sauce, tamari or Bragg Aminos

125ml/4floz (½ cup) sweet chilli sauce

½ tsp chilli flakes (or to taste)

2 tsp garam masala

2 tsp curry powder

Add-Ins:

400g/14oz can chickpeas, drained

120g/4oz baby spinach leaves

400g/14oz can diced tomatoes

INSTRUCTIONS

1 Blend sauce ingredients in a blender for about half a minute until smooth and well combined.

2 Place sauce and adds-ins into a small pot and heat over medium to high heat. Stir constantly and turn heat down to a simmer. Cover with a lid and let simmer for 5 to 10 minutes to infuse the flavors.

 RECIPE NOTES

Add ½ cup of raisins for a fruity kick.

POTATO & PEA CURRY

Serves: 1 without sides | 2 with sides

Suggested Sides: rice or Naan bread

INGREDIENTS

320g/11oz potatoes, diced very small (pinky fingertip sized)

2 cups frozen peas

2 tsp onion granules

1 tsp ground coriander

1 tsp curry powder

1 tsp ground cumin

1 tsp coarse celtic sea salt

3 tsp tamari or soy sauce

¼ cup coconut milk

1 cup boiled water

INSTRUCTIONS

1 Place potatoes, peas and spices in a pot and put onto high heat. Stir constantly for a couple of minutes to mix everything and to stop it from sticking to the bottom of the pot.

2 Next pour in the tamari, coconut milk and water and stir through again. Keep on medium to high heat so that it continues at a low boil.

3 Cover with a lid and cook for 10 minutes until the potatoes are soft.

SWEET POTATO & LENTIL CURRY

Serves: 2 without sides | 4 with sides

Suggested Sides: rice or Naan bread

INGREDIENTS

500g/17.5oz (4 small) sweet potatoes, diced very small (pinky fingertip sized)

400g/14oz can lentils (not drained)

1 tsp onion granules

1 tsp onion powder

1 tsp ground coriander

1 tsp ground cumin

½ tsp cinnamon

¼ cup raisins

3 tsp tamari or soy sauce

¼ cup coconut milk

½ cup boiled water

INSTRUCTIONS

1 Place all of the ingredients in a pot and put onto high heat. Stir constantly for a couple of minutes to mix everything together.

2 Turn heat down to keep the pot at a high simmer.

3 Cover with a lid and cook for 10 minutes until the sweet potatoes are soft.

RECIPE NOTES

Add cubed tofu when you are feeling extra hungry!

CREAMY VEGETABLE & MUSHROOM CURRY

Serves: 1 without sides | 2 with sides

Suggested Sides: rice or Naan bread

INGREDIENTS

300g/10.5oz frozen vegetables (I used a mix of broccoli, carrots and corn)

200g/7oz sliced mushrooms

Sauce:

¼ cup peanut butter

⅛ tsp white pepper

1 tbsp curry powder

½ cup cooked chickpeas

1 tsp coconut sugar

½ tsp coarse celtic sea salt

1 tbsp tamari or soy sauce

1 cup water

INSTRUCTIONS

1 Place the vegetables and mushrooms in a pot.

2 Blend all of the sauce ingredients for about 1 minute until smooth and creamy. Then pour sauce into the pot.

3 Turn heat to high and stir constantly until mixture just starts to bubble.

4 Reduce heat to a simmer, cover with a lid and leave to cook for about 10 minutes.

 RECIPE NOTES

Add cubed tofu when you are feeling extra hungry!

THAI GREEN PEANUT CURRY NOODLES

Serves: 1 without sides | 2 with sides

Suggested Sides: rice or rice noodles

INGREDIENTS

1 small onion, sliced lengthways

2 zucchinis (450g/16oz)

1 tbsp green curry paste (or adjust depending on brand and heat level)

3 tsp soy sauce

½ cup coconut milk

3 tsp peanut butter

1 tsp coconut sugar

¼ cup fresh Thai basil leaves, optional

Salt and pepper to taste

RECIPE NOTES

Great served with chopped peanuts or cashews on top. Add tofu to make this a heartier meal. If you want a lower fat version, use a low fat plant milk and add coconut extract for the coconut flavor.

INSTRUCTIONS

1 Heat a pot on medium to high heat.

2 Add onion and zucchini and stir. Once onion starts to brown, add a dash of water to deglaze the pan.

3 Add the curry paste and soy sauce, then stir until the paste is mixed through.

4 Now add the remaining ingredients and stir to make sure everything is combined well.

5 Lower the heat and continue simmering for about 5 minutes until the zucchini has softened and the sauce has reduced.

6 Place the curry into serving bowl and enjoy!

CHILI CON BEANS

Serves: 1 without sides | 2 with sides

Suggested Sides: rice, pasta or crusty bread

INGREDIENTS

1 tsp onion powder

1 tsp garlic powder

½ tsp chili flakes, or to taste

1 tsp paprika

1 tsp cumin

400g/14oz can red kidney beans, drained

½ cup chargrilled red peppers strips/capsicum (I used pickled and drained from a jar)

¼ cup BBQ sauce

400g/14oz can diced tomatoes (including juices)

Salt and pepper to taste

INSTRUCTIONS

1 Place everything into a pot and bring to the boil.

2 Lower heat and simmer for about 10-12 minutes until the sauce reduces a bit and the beans soften.

ASIAN TERIYAKI NOODLE BOWL

Serves: 1

INGREDIENTS

220g/8oz rice noodles (pre-cooked or soaked in hot water for 5 minutes)

1 cup vegetable stock

1 cup boiled water

2 tbsp teriyaki sauce

1 cup sliced mushrooms

1 nori sheet, crumbled

¼ cup/small handful fresh coriander leaves (or herb of choice)

Optional: pickled ginger, spring onions, sliced chilli, baby corn, bok choi, Asian greens, cubed tofu

INSTRUCTIONS

1 Place noodles, mushrooms, nori, herbs and optional vegetables in a flat bowl. Pour over half the teriyaki sauce, vegetable stock and the boiled water.

2 Let sit for a few minutes till vegetables are softened.

3 Drizzle with remaining teriyaki sauce and extra fresh herbs of your choice.

 RECIPE NOTES

To make this extra warm, put everything into a pot and gently heat for 5 minutes.

MUSHROOM AND CORN RICE

Serves: 2

INGREDIENTS

1 small onion, diced
100g/3.5oz firm mushrooms (eg. shiitake, oyster - see recipe note)
80g/3oz corn kernels
1 cup frozen peas
1 cup rice, uncooked
2 cups vegetable stock
Salt and pepper to taste
Serve with: a squeeze of fresh lemon and a small handful fresh parsley for garnish

INSTRUCTIONS

1 Dry fry onion and rice for 2 minutes in a pot or pan.

2 Add a splash of the vegetable stock and the mushrooms and stir for 1 minute.

3 Add remaining ingredients and stir occasionally to prevent sticking.

4 Cook for approximately 10 minutes till done.

5 Serve topped with a squeeze of lemon juice and fresh parsley.

 RECIPE NOTES

Break mushrooms into bite size pieces rather than cutting to keep good texture and to give them a "chewy" mouthfeel. Great served with sliced avocado.

SWEET CORN BREAD DUMPLING STEW

Serves: 2

INGREDIENTS

Soup
2 cups vegetable stock
250g/9oz corn kernels
400g/14oz can cannellini beans, drained
2 tbsp nutritional yeast flakes, optional

Dumplings
2 slices bread, torn into pieces
1 tsp dried onion flakes
1 tsp mixed dried Italian herbs
Dash white pepper
3 tbsp chickpea/besan/garbanzo flour
½ cup water
1 tbsp flax meal

INSTRUCTIONS

Soup

1 Place all soup ingredients into a pot and put on medium to high heat.

2 Now make the dumplings. Mix all dumpling ingredients in a bowl & roll into small walnut size balls.

3 Place dumplings into the simmering liquid and cook about 8 minutes till cooked through.

TAGINE QUINOA ONE POT

Serves: 2

Suggested Sides: crusty bread

INGREDIENTS

1 cup/185g/6.5oz quinoa, uncooked

2 cups hot water, boiled in kettle

400g/14oz can diced tomatoes, including juices

400g/14 oz can chickpeas/garbanzo beans, drained

2 zucchinis, diced (approx 450g/16oz)

1 tbsp ground dry cumin

1 tbsp ground dry coriander/cilantro

2 tsp cumin seeds, optional

1 tbsp lemon juice - mix through at the end

Fresh chopped herbs for garnish

Salt and pepper to taste

INSTRUCTIONS

1 Place everything into a pot with a lid and bring to the boil.

2 Lower heat and simmer with lid on for about 10-12 minutes until quinoa is soft and vegetables cooked through.

PEA AND MUSHROOM MEDITERRANEAN PASTA

Serves: 2

Suggested Sides: crusty bread and a crispy green salad

INGREDIENTS

2 cups sliced mushrooms
1 cup frozen peas
125g/4.5oz uncooked pasta (any type you like)
400g/14oz can diced tomatoes
¼ cup mild salsa (from jar)
400g/14oz can beans, drained (I used cannellini beans)
1 cup vegetable stock
1 cup extra water
Salt and pepper to taste

INSTRUCTIONS

1 Get medium sized pot with a lid and place in all of the ingredients (except extra water) prior to putting on the heat.

2 Give everything a good stir through and turn the heat to high and stir occasionally until it comes to a light boil. Maintain heat and keep at a light boil for about 5 minutes. Stir again.

3 Add extra water and turn heat down to a simmer and cook for 8-12 minutes until the pasta is cooked through. Remove from heat and let the mixture sit for a few minutes. It will thicken once off heat.

SWEET POTATO BEANS WITH CREAMY PARSLEY SAUCE

Serves: 2

Suggested Sides: rice, pasta or crusty bread

INGREDIENTS

400g/14oz can cannellini beans, drained

250g/9oz sweet potato, sliced into discs

1 tsp onion flakes

150g/5oz green beans

½ cup plant milk

1 handful fresh parsley

½ - 1 tsp coarse celtic sea salt (adjust to your taste)

1 tbsp sliced spring onion

INSTRUCTIONS

1 Place quarter of the cannellini beans in a pot of water with the sweet potato, onion flakes and green beans and boil on high for 10 minutes, then strain. (see recipe note)

2 In the meantime, blend all of the remaining ingredients to make your parsley sauce.

3 Serve your cooked vegetables with the sauce over the top.

 RECIPE NOTES

For more sauce, keep the boiling liquid and add to the blender mixture. Thicken with cornflour/cornstarch.

"CHEESY" CORN PASTA

Serves: 1 without sides | 2 with sides

Suggested Sides: crusty bread and crispy fresh salad, steamed vegetables such

INGREDIENTS

100g/3.5oz dry pasta (any type you like)

180g/6oz corn kernels (divided in 2)

70g/2.5oz blanched almonds

1 tbsp white miso paste (or tahini mixed with soy sauce)

2 tbsp nutritional yeast flakes

1 tsp onion powder

250ml/8.5floz plant milk

2 tsp cornflour/cornstarch

Salt and pepper to taste

INSTRUCTIONS

1 Cook pasta as per packet instructions.

2 Blend everything (except for pasta and half of the corn kernels) until smooth and creamy.

3 Pour the sauce over the drained pasta and mix through the remaining corn kernels.

4 Serve immediately!

SUPER QUICK "CHEESY" MAC PASTA

Serves: 2 without sides | 4 with sides

Suggested Sides: crusty bread, steamed vegetables, or crispy fresh salad

INGREDIENTS

250g uncooked pasta of choice * keep drained cooking water for sauce!

Sauce

1 cup cashews/chickpeas (or 2 cups cooked cauliflower)

1 clove garlic

½ tsp coarse celtic sea salt

Dash white pepper

¼ cup nutritional yeast flakes

2 tbsp chopped roasted red bell peppers/ capsicums (I used pickled and drained from jar)

½ cup plant milk

INSTRUCTIONS

1 Cook pasta as per packet instructions.

2 Blend all sauce ingredients while pasta is cooking.

3 Drain pasta but don't rinse (and reserve about ½ cup of the cooking liquid).

4 Place pasta back in the pot and add sauce (and some of the cooking liquid as needed to make it more creamy and gooey). Mix everything together and serve!

CITRUS SPIKED PUMPKIN & LENTIL RISOTTO

Serves: 2

INGREDIENTS

1 cup rice (Aborio or medium grain white rice)

1 cup vegetable stock

1 cup plant milk, I used soy

1 tsp onion powder

1 tsp garlic powder

1 cup/150g/5oz pumpkin or squash/sweet potato, chopped into small cubes (index finger sized)

400g/14oz can brown lentils, drained (220g/8oz drained weight)

Add-ins once cooked:

1 cup fresh chopped parsley

Fresh lemon juice, to taste

Salt and pepper, to taste

INSTRUCTIONS

1 Add all ingredients to a small pot with lid. Bring to boil and then lower heat to simmer.

2 Stir every few minutes to prevent sticking and put lid back on each time.

3 Simmer for 10-15 minutes until rice and pumpkin are soft.

4 Serve with fresh parsley mixed through. Squeeze fresh lemon juice over the top and season with salt and pepper. Dig in!

Flashes in the Pan

Teriyaki Maple Glazed Tofu & Eggplant Stir Fry pg.35

Corn Fritters p.38

Quick & Easy Satay Noodles p.42

KALE AND OYSTER MUSHROOMS WITH GRILLED CORN

Serves: 1 without sides | 2 with sides

Suggested Sides: rice, avocado, crusty bread, steamed vegetables

INGREDIENTS

100g/3.5oz oyster mushrooms (or any mushrooms of your choice)

1 tbsp finely sliced scallions

2 cups finely chopped kale leaves

1 tsp dried onion flakes

½ tsp grated lemon rind

¼ cup vegetable stock

1 corn cob, cut into chunks

Fresh lemon juice and coriander to serve

INSTRUCTIONS

1 Bring a non-stick frying pan to high heat.

2 Add in mushrooms, spring onion kales leaves, onion flakes and lemon rind.

3 Stir and cook using vegetable stock to deglaze pan as needed.

4 In the meantime, bake or grill corn to brown lightly.

5 Serve immediately with freshly squeezed lemon and coriander over the top!

TERIYAKI MAPLE GLAZED TOFU & EGGPLANT STIR FRY

Serves: 1 without sides | 2 with sides

Suggested Sides: rice or quinoa

INGREDIENTS

200g/7oz firm tofu, cubed

100g/3.5oz pre-cut stir fry vegetables (I used store bought)

100g/3.5oz eggplant, cut into very small cubes

1 tbsp teriyaki sauce

2 tbsp maple syrup

2 tbsp water + 1 tbsp cornstarch (mixed together in a small bowl or jar)

Optional toppings: fresh sliced chilli, spring onions and flaked almonds

Salt and pepper to taste

INSTRUCTIONS

1 Bring a non-stick frying pan to high heat.

2 Add everything except optional toppings to the pan.

3 Stir and cook until eggplant has softened and everything is hot and cooked through.

4 Top with optional extras and season to taste.

 RECIPE NOTES

If you have time, place eggplant in boiling water to soften prior to placing in the pan. This takes away the bitter taste that eggplant can sometimes have, especially if not super fresh.

SAVORY FILLED OMELETTE

Serves: 1

Suggested Sides: crusty fresh bread

INGREDIENTS

⅔ cup water

¼ cup chickpea/besan flour

1 tbsp ground flax seeds (flax meal)

1 tbsp nutritional yeast flakes, optional

¼ tsp baking powder

¼ tsp black salt, optional - adds an egg flavor

¼ tsp white pepper

⅛ tsp turmeric

⅛ tsp coarse celtic sea salt

⅛ tsp garlic powder

⅛ tsp chilli flakes

Suggested Toppings/ Fillings:

Mushrooms, spinach, char-grilled red peppers, pesto, hummus, potatoes etc

INSTRUCTIONS

1 For this recipe it is nice to have a blender, however, you can mix the ingredients manually. You will also need a medium sized non stick pan with a lid (preferably glass so you can see how it is cooking).

2 Place the ingredients into your blender and blend till smooth.

3 Pour the mixture into the pan and place on a low to medium heat. Cover the pan with a lid for 3-4 minutes until the top of the omelette has a sponge-like consistency (quite firm on top like bread).

4 From here you can either fold in your favorite ingredients and serve or turn over the omelette to brown both sides.

POTATO PANCAKES

Serves: makes 8-12 pancakes depending on size

Suggested Sides: avocado, steamed vegetables, hummus, crispy salad

INGREDIENTS

2 medium potatoes
(325g/11.5oz)
1 onion (100g/3.5oz)
1 cup flour (plain or
gluten free)
1 tsp baking powder
1 tsp coarse celtic sea salt
⅛ tsp ground black
pepper
1 cup water

INSTRUCTIONS

1 Place everything in a blender and blend till roughly processed.

2 Heat a non-stick pan to medium and cook in small batches until all pancakes are done.

3 Top with optional extras and season to taste.

 RECIPE NOTES

For a sweet version, swap onion for an extra potato and serve with apple sauce and fresh fruit.

CORN FRITTERS

Serves: makes 16 fritters

Suggested Sides: avocado, hummus, steamed vegetables, crispy salad

INGREDIENTS

1 extra large zucchini (375g/12oz)

½ cup whole wheat flour (or flour of choice)

2 tsp dried onion flakes

1 tsp coarse celtic sea salt

¼ tsp white pepper

2 tsp mixed Italian herbs, dried

½ cup chickpea/besan flour

2 corn cobs, kernels

½ cup water

chilli flakes, optional to taste

INSTRUCTIONS

1 Mix all ingredients (except water) together in a bowl.

2 Add water and mix again.

3 Spoon into medium-hot non stick frying pan and cook a few minutes on each side until cooked through.

4 You can place them in the oven to keep warm... or eat straight away! YUM!

VEGETABLE LOADED FRIED RICE

Serves: 1 without sides | 2 with sides

Suggested Sides: avocado and steamed vegetables

INGREDIENTS

2 cups cooked rice

1 small rib of celery, sliced thinly

1 large kale leaf (no stalk), chopped small

1 small onion, sliced or diced

2 tbsp spring onion, sliced

¼ red bell pepper, diced small

½ cup peas (I use frozen)

4 slices lemon

⅛ cup water

Salt and pepper to taste

Stir Fry Sauce

¼ cup vegetable stock

1 tbsp tamari or soy sauce

1 tsp sriracha/hot sauce, optional

1 tsp maple syrup

Optional Toppings:

handful of peanuts or cashews, sesame seeds, fresh basil or coriander.

INSTRUCTIONS

1. Place lemon slices in a hot non-stick frying pan with a splash of water. Allow juice to release a bit and then remove (use them for garnish later if you wish).

2. Add vegetables and water to the pan and stir through for a few minutes until vegetables start to soften.

3. Add rice and sauce ingredients and continue to stir until everything is cooked through and well combined.

 RECIPE NOTES

I like to use basmati rice. To cook mine I bring water to the boil with a vegetable stock cube or a dash of coarse celtic sea salt. Place washed rice in the boiling water and boil for 8 minutes. Remove and strain immediately. Let cool a little and fluff it up with a fork. Delicious!

HOISIN & BLACK SESAME RICE NOODLES

Serves: 2

INGREDIENTS

300g/10.5oz sliced mushrooms

500g/17.5oz frozen vegetables (Asian stir fry style)

220g/8oz pre-cooked rice noodles

2 tbsp Hoisin sauce

1 tbsp tamari or soy sauce

1 tbsp black sesame seeds

Fresh cracked pepper to serve

INSTRUCTIONS

1 Place everything except the noodles and sesame seeds in a hot non-stick frypan. Stir for a minute, lower the heat to medium and put a lid on.

2 Place noodles in a colander and run hot water over them for a minute to soften and heat them slightly.

3 Toss noodles into the frypan and stir for a couple of minutes on medium to high heat.

4 Serve topped with freshly cracked pepper and sesame seeds.

RECIPE NOTES

Add tofu or black beans for extra iron, texture and bulk.

"CHICKEN" STYLE RISSOLES

Serves: 2 - 4 with sides

Suggested Sides: crusty bread, steamed vegetables, crispy salad

INGREDIENTS

2 slices bread (stale is fine)
½ cup rice bubbles
1 tbsp onion flakes
1 tbsp dried chives
¼ tsp white pepper
75g/3oz oyster mushrooms, sliced
⅓ cup chickpea/besan flour
½ tsp vegetable stock powder (I like to use Massel "chicken style")
½ cup vegetable stock

INSTRUCTIONS

1 Tear up the bread and combine with all other ingredients in a mixing bowl.

2 Using your hands, knead everything together and then shape into 4 patties.

3 Cook in a medium to hot non stick frypan till cooked through.

 RECIPE NOTES

Cover your pan with a lid to help the patties cook through faster. Almost like steam cooking them and then finish them off without the lid to make the outsides slightly crispy. You could also bake them in the oven!

QUICK & EASY SATAY NOODLES

Serves: 1 without sides | 2 with sides

Suggested Sides: steamed vegetables

INGREDIENTS

2 handfuls of mixed crunchy pre-chopped stir fry vegetables

220g/8oz packet pre-cooked rice noodles

Satay Sauce

¼ cup peanut butter (I prefer smooth)

2 tbsp sweet chilli sauce

1 tbsp tamari/soy sauce/coconut aminos

¼ cup water

Optional Toppings:

Fresh basil leaves, roasted peanuts and a lime wedge to squeeze over the top

INSTRUCTIONS

1. Place all sauce ingredients in a small bowl or jar with a lid and shake until well combined.

2. Heat a non-stick frypan on high and toss in the vegetables. Use a splash of water to stop them from sticking (like you would if you were using oil).

3. Once the vegetables have softened to your liking, add in the noodles and the sauce and stir for a couple more minutes.

ORANGE PEANUT FLAT RICE NOODLES

Serves: 1 without sides | 2 with sides

Suggested Sides: steamed vegetables, tofu

INGREDIENTS

1 handful roasted cashews or peanuts

½ cup sliced scallions

¼ cup red bell pepper/capsicum, sliced

1 cup small broccoli pieces

100g/3.5oz pre-cooked flat rice noodles

Sauce

1 cup orange juice

1 tbsp tamari/soy sauce/coconut aminos

½ cup peanut butter

1 tbsp coconut cream

1 tbsp cornstarch

½ tsp coarse celtic sea salt

Optional Toppings:

Roasted cashew and chilli flakes or fresh sliced chilli

INSTRUCTIONS

1 Whisk together the sauce ingredients in a bowl and set aside.

2 In a hot non-stick frypan, stir fry the nuts and vegetables with a splash of water.

3 Add in the rice noodles and toss through to combine.

4 Pour over the sauce and stir through for another minute or two.

5 Serve with any optional toppings that you like.

LENTIL BOLOGNESE

Serves: 2

Suggested Sides: crusty bread, steamed vegetables, crispy salad

INGREDIENTS

100g/3.5oz (dry weight) macaroni

1 medium carrot, grated

1 small onion, grated

2 cloves garlic, minced

400g/14oz can brown lentils, drained and rinsed

1 cup passata (or Italian tomato cooking sauce of your choice)

½ cup water (or red wine)

Add-ins:

Handful of fresh chopped parsley

INSTRUCTIONS

1 Cook macaroni as per packet instructions.

2 Cook carrot, onion and garlic over medium to high heat in a non-stick frypan. Use a splash of water if it starts to stick.

3 Add remaining ingredients and lower the heat.

4 Simmer for 10 minutes or till cooked to your liking.

5 Season with salt and pepper and stir through a handful of fresh parsley.

6 Serve with your cooked and drained macaroni. YUM!

CAULIFLOWER IN LEMON SAUCE WITH RICE

Serves: 2

Suggested Sides: steamed vegetables, baked tofu

INGREDIENTS

2-4 cups cooked rice
1 small head cauliflower, broken into small florets

Sauce
1 cup vegetable stock
1 small lemon, zest and juice
2 tbsp maple syrup
1 tsp coarse celtic sea salt
1 tbsp cornstarch
1 cloves garlic, minced

Optional Topping:
Sesame seeds

INSTRUCTIONS

1 Mix all of the sauce ingredients together in a bowl or a screw top jar and set aside.

2 Stir fry the cauliflower in a medium to hot non stick frypan using a splash of water to stop it from burning.

3 Once softened, add the sauce and cook for another couple of minutes until it is slightly thick and sticky.

4 Remove from heat and serve with rice and any additional extras that you like.

GREEN BOOSTED TOFU SCRAMBLE

Serves: 2

Suggested Sides: crusty bread, baked sweet potato, avocado, steamed vegetables

INGREDIENTS

200g/7oz firm tofu, crumbled
½ tsp turmeric powder
1 tsp onion flakes
2 tsp dried chives
¼ tsp black salt (tastes eggy)
1 tbsp tamari or soy sauce
Handful chopped kales leaves (or baby spinach leaves)
Salt and pepper to taste
Extra water for thinning out and oil free cooking!

Optional
Squeeze fresh lemon over the top and sprinkle with freshly chopped parsley or any herbs of your choice

INSTRUCTIONS

1 Place all of the ingredients except the extra water into a non-stick frypan and stir everything together in the pan before putting it onto the heat.

2 Place on medium to high heat and add splashes of water to stop sticking and to make everything combine together properly.

3 Top with optional extras and serve!

 RECIPE NOTES

You could also add sliced mushrooms to the mix!

STIR FRIED GREEN CURRY NOODLES

Serves: 2

Suggested Sides: steamed vegetables, baked tofu, rice

INGREDIENTS

¼ cup vegetable stock
1 tbsp green curry paste
1 handful green beans (about 15)
¼ red bell pepper/capsicum, sliced
2 tbsp scallions, sliced
1 tbsp tamari/soy sauce/coconut aminos
¼ cup coconut milk
2 tbsp fresh
Thai basil leaves
220g/8oz packet wok-ready rice noodles

Optional Toppings:
Peanuts, cashews, flaked almonds, fresh coriander, lime wedge

INSTRUCTIONS

1 Heat a non-stick frying pan on high heat.

2 Add a splash of the vegetable stock and the curry paste and stir for a minute or so till fragrant.

3 Add remaining ingredients (except coconut milk, basil and noodles).

4 Lower heat to medium and simmer about 5 minutes until the vegetables are tender.

5 Add coconut milk, basil and noodles and cook for a few more minutes until heated through. Enjoy!

CORN AND POTATO PANCAKE BREAD

Serves: 1 without sides | 2 with sides

Suggested Sides: steamed vegetables, crispy salad, baked tofu

INGREDIENTS

2 potatoes, grated
¼ cup corn kernels
1 tbsp dried chives
3 tbsp cornstarch
½ cup Pan
(yellow corn meal)

Fresh Toppings:
Cucumber, avocado, passata tomato sauce, BBQ sauce, red bell peppers/capsicums, fresh herbs, cashew sour cream

INSTRUCTIONS

1 Form all of the ingredients into a dough.

2 Roll into a large pancake shape.

3 Place into a large nonstick frypan and cook on medium high heat for about 5 minutes on each side.

4 Put on a plate and top with any additional extras that you like.

 RECIPE NOTES

You could also portion into 4 or 6 and make smaller pan cakes.

RED LENTIL PANCAKES WITH CREAMED BEETROOT

Serves: 1 without sides | 2 with sides

Suggested Sides: steamed vegetables, crispy salad, avocado

INGREDIENTS

⅓ cup pink split lentils, washed

½ cup water

½ tsp coarse celtic sea salt

¼ tsp baking powder

1 clove garlic

2 tsp nutritional yeast flakes, optional

⅛ small onion

Dash white pepper

Creamed Beetroot

150g/5oz beetroot, washed and grated (I left skin on mine)

1 tsp lemon juice

1 tbsp tahini

1 tbsp water

Salt and pepper to taste

INSTRUCTIONS

1 Blend the main ingredients until fairly smooth pancake batter consistency is reached.

2 Divide batter into two or four and cook your lentil pancakes in a nonstick frypan over medium heat on each side.

3 For the creamed beetroot, simply mix the ingredients in a bowl and then serve on top of your pancakes once they are cooked and ready to eat. YUM!

 RECIPE NOTES

Top with fresh chopped parsley or cilantro, a lemon wedge and a sprinkling of sesame seeds!

CREAMY VEGAN "SEAFOOD" MARINARA

Serves: 2

Suggested Sides: crusty bread, steamed vegetables, crispy salad

INGREDIENTS

250g/9oz gnocchi, pre-cooked

2 large king oyster mushrooms (200g/7oz)

2 tbsp sliced sundried tomatoes

Sauce

1 cup passata (or Italian cooking sauce of your choice)

¼ to ⅓ cup plant milk

Salt and pepper to taste

INSTRUCTIONS

1 Cut the stems of the mushrooms into disk shapes and then use round cookie cutters to cut into "calamari" style circles.

2 Cut the top into thick strips or in half to mimic oysters.

3 Place the mushrooms in a hot non-stick pan and use splashes of water to stop them from sticking while they cook for a few minutes to soften.

4 Add in the gnocchi and sauce ingredients and lower the heat.

5 Simmer for about 5 minutes and enjoy!

COCONUT GINGER BRUSSELS SPROUTS

Serves: 1 without sides | 2 with sides

Suggested Sides: rice or quinoa

INGREDIENTS

400g/14oz can chickpeas, drained
1 clove garlic, minced
½ small onion, grated
1 thumb sized piece of ginger, sliced or minced
200g/7oz Brussels sprouts, quartered
1 tbsp soy sauce

Sauce

¼ cup vegetable stock
2 tbsp coconut cream
1 tbsp lemon juice

Add In:

1 large handful of chopped cilantro or Thai basil

INSTRUCTIONS

1 Pan fry the main ingredients using splashes of water if needed to prevent sticking.

2 Add sauce ingredients and stir through.

3 Take off the heat and stir through fresh herbs.

 RECIPE NOTES

Top with dry roasted coconut (2 tbsp dried coconut cooked in a non-stick frypan for a few minutes on high heat until crispy and browned).

SPICY TOFU CHORIZO AND BLACK BEAN RICE

Serves: 2

Suggested Sides: avocado, steamed vegetables

INGREDIENTS

150g/5oz firm tofu
1 tbsp tamari/soy sauce/coconut aminos
1 tbsp dried onion flakes
1 tbsp smoked paprika
½ - 1 tsp dried chilli flakes
1 tsp ground cinnamon
1 tsp ground cumin
1 tsp coarse celtic sea salt
¼ tsp ground black pepper
½ tsp liquid smoke (I use hickory flavored)

Add-ins:
400g/14oz can black beans, drained
2 cups cooked rice

INSTRUCTIONS

1. Crumble the tofu into small bits (ground beef consistency) and into a frying pan before placing it on the heat.

2. Add all of the main ingredients to the pan and stir through to combine everything well, then put pan on medium to high heat.

3. Stir for a few minutes to heat everything well and until the tofu starts to get a bit crispy on the edges.

4. Add beans and rice to the pan and stir through until everything is well combined and heated nicely.

WAITROSE

& PARTNERS

RECIPE

SPINACH PASTA WITH SAVOY CABBAGE & GORGONZOLA

SPINACH PASTA WITH SAVOY CABBAGE & GORGONZOLA

Serves 4 | **Prepare** 10 minutes | **Cook** 15 minutes

Ingredients

- 1 tbsp olive oil
- 2 echalion shallots, finely sliced
- 2 garlic cloves, crushed
- 1 tsp honey
- 1 small savoy cabbage, shredded
- ½ lemon, zest, plus a squeeze of juice to serve
- **250g Seeds of Change Organic Spinach Trottole Pasta**
- 75g gorgonzola piccante, cut into small pieces

Method

1 Heat the oil in a large, wide pan set over a medium heat and fry the shallots for 8 minutes until lightly golden. Stir in the garlic and cook for 1 minute, then add the honey, cabbage and 3 tbsp water; fry for another 3-4 minutes until just wilted. Add the lemon zest and season.

2 Meanwhile, simmer the pasta in a pan of boiling salted water for 8 minutes. Scoop out a cupful of the cooking liquid, then drain. Tip the pasta into the wide pan with 3 tbsp of the cooking liquid; toss everything together over a high heat. Fold through the gorgonzola, check the seasoning and serve immediately with a squeeze of lemon juice.

Per serving 1749kJ/433kcals/11.3g fat/4.8g saturated fat/62.2g carbs/ 9.2g sugars/7.9g fibre/16.6g protein/0.85g salt

Cook's tip

For added crunch, sprinkle some roughly chopped toasted hazelnuts over the top of the pasta.

And to drink...

Pair with the zesty and vibrant **Waitrose & Partners Blueprint Gavi**, Piedmont, Italy, 75cl

drinkaware.co.uk for the facts

SATAY SKEWERS

Serves: 1 without sides | 2 with sides

Suggested Sides: rice, steamed vegetables, crispy salad

INGREDIENTS

250g/9oz king oyster mushrooms, sliced lengthways (size of small finger is best)

1 tbsp peanut butter

½ tsp sambal oelek (chilli paste)

½ tsp garlic, minced

2 tsp soy sauce

1 tsp maple syrup

1 tbsp hot boiled water

INSTRUCTIONS

1 Thread mushrooms strips onto bamboo or metal skewers.

2 Mix the remaining ingredients together until thick and creamy.

3 Rub the mushroom skewers with the sauce mixture and cook on medium to high heat on all sides until lightly browned.

4 Serve with steamed rice and vegetables for a quick and tasty meal!

 RECIPE NOTES

Double the sauce and use half for marinade and half to serve.

Salads And Wraps

Pearl Couscous Salad pg.59

Mushroom & Sweet Potato Wrap with Cauliflower Miso Cream pg. 60

Mexican Salad Bowl pg.66

ASIAN STYLE SWEET POTATO AND GREEN BEAN SALAD

Serves: 2 without sides | 4 with sides

Suggested Sides: rice, steamed vegetables, baked tofu

INGREDIENTS

1 large sweet potato, cubed into thumb sized pieces

250g/9oz green beans

Dressing

1 stalk scallion, sliced diagonally

1 tbsp lime juice

1 tbsp tamari/soy sauce/ coconut aminos

1 tbsp maple syrup

1 tbsp almond butter or tahini

1 tbsp hot water (from steaming vegetable or boiled from kettle)

Optional Toppings:

slivered almonds, sesame seeds

INSTRUCTIONS

1 Steam sweet potato and green beans until tender.

2 In the meantime mix all of the dressing ingredients in a jar with a screw top lid and shake it up to mix it through thoroughly.

3 Either let the vegetables cool down or serve the salad warm. Place in a bowl or on a platter and pour over the dressing. Finally add the optional toppings if you wish.

ANTIPASTO POTATO SALAD

Serves: 2 without sides | 4 with sides

Suggested Sides: crusty bread, steamed vegetables, baked tofu

INGREDIENTS

300g/10.5oz cooked potatoes (I like to use kipflers)

275g/10oz jar artichoke hearts, roughly drained

140g/5oz chargrilled vegetables (I used eggplant, zucchini etc from jar)

½ cup whole olives of your choice (or ¼ cup sliced)

¼ cup sundried tomatoes

¼ cup chargrilled red bell peppers/capsicums (I used pickled ones from jar)

INSTRUCTIONS

1 Slice, dice or quarter your cooked potatoes into whatever shapes you like and combine in a bowl with all of the remaining ingredients. That's it... easiest potato salad ever!

CREAMY CURRIED LENTIL AND MACARONI PASTA SALAD

Serves: 2 without sides | 4 with sides

Suggested Sides: steamed vegetables, baked tofu, avocado

INGREDIENTS

1 cup dry macaroni
(or 2 cups of cooked
macaroni)
1 cup frozen peas
400g/14oz can brown
lentils, drained

Sauce
½ tsp curry powder
½ cup cashews
½ - 1 tsp coarse celtic sea salt
¼ cup water
1 small clove garlic
1tbs lemon juice

INSTRUCTIONS

1 Cook pasta as per packet instructions and add peas to boiling pot a few minutes before pasta is done. Drain, but do not rinse.

2 Blend all of the sauce ingredients in a blender until smooth and creamy.

3 Place pasta and sauce into a salad bowl, mix and serve.

 RECIPE NOTES

Great with 1 or 2 handfuls of raisins for a slightly sweet highlight!

PEARL COUSCOUS SALAD

Serves: 2

Suggested Sides: steamed vegetables, avocado, baked sweet potato, baked tofu

INGREDIENTS

125g pearl couscous

Add-Ins:
½ small cabbage sliced
1 handful fresh herbs
(I used cilantro)
¼ cup frozen peas (put
under hot water to thaw
for a minute or so)
1 tbsp dried chives

Dressing
½ cup tahini
¼ cup lemon juice
1-2 garlic cloves, minced
1 tsp coarse celtic sea salt
2 - 4 tbsp water

INSTRUCTIONS

1 Cook pearl couscous as per packet instructions.

2 In the meantime, place all of the add-ins into a salad bowl.

3 To make the dressing, whisk all dressing ingredients except water together in a small bowl. Add a bit of the water as needed to thin out to the consistency that you like.

4 Add cooked couscous and dressing to the bowl and stir gently to combine and mix through. Enjoy!

MUSHROOM & SWEET POTATO WRAP WITH CAULIFLOWER MISO CREAM

Serves: 1

Suggested Sides: steamed vegetables, crispy salad, baked tofu, avocado

INGREDIENTS

1 large portobello
mushroom, sliced
1 cup sweet potato cubes,
thumb sized
½ cup vegetable stock
½ tbs dried onion flakes
1 tbsp dried chives

Sauce

1 cup cauliflower pieces
1 clove garlic
¼ - ½ cup vegetable stock
(depending on how
moist the cauliflower is)
1 tsp white miso paste
1 tsp dijon mustard

Optional Toppings:

Mushroom, sweet potato
and extra salad, beans,
tofu etc

INSTRUCTIONS

1   Cook all of the main ingredients
in a hot non-stick fry pan until
mushrooms are softened and cooked
through. Add splashes of water if
need to deglaze the plan.

2   In the meantime boil cauliflower
pieces and garlic clove for about
7 minutes till soft. Drain once cooked.

3   Blend cooked cauliflower and garlic
with remaining sauce ingredients.

4   Top your wrap with the sauce and
mushrooms.

5   Add any extra toppings that you like.

POTATO AND GREEN BEAN SALAD

Serves: 2 without sides | 4 with sides

Suggested Sides: crusty bread, avocado, steamed vegetables, baked tofu

INGREDIENTS

250g/9oz potato, sliced into disks
1 handful green beans
1 small carrot, sliced
1 tbsp dried chives
400g/14oz can cannellini beans, drained

Dressing
1 tbs lemon juice
1 tbsp maple syrup
1 tbsp dijon mustard
1 tsp soy sauce

Salt and pepper to taste
Scallions to garnish

INSTRUCTIONS

1 Boil all of the main ingredients till tender and drain once done.

2 Mix dressing ingredients well to combine.

3 Place everything into a salad bowl and toss gently to combine.

4 Garnish with scallions and enjoy!

FRUITY RICE SALAD WITH PINEAPPLE ALMOND DRESSING

Serves: 2

Suggested Sides: fruit bread, fresh fruit

INGREDIENTS

2 cup cooked rice
½ large carrot, grated
1 apple, cubed
1 banana sliced
1 tbsp lemon juice
½ cup canned pineapple, drained (reserve juice)

Pineapple Almond Dressing

2 tbsp almond butter (or peanut butter)
2 tbsp maple syrup
¼ tsp coarse celtic sea salt
2 tbsp water
¼ cup pineapple juice

Extra

1 cup plant milk

INSTRUCTIONS

1 Place everything except plant milk into a bowl and mix well.

2 Take one cup of the salad mix and blend with 1 cup plant milk.

3 Pour this thick sauce mixture over the salad to make it extra creamy.

 RECIPE NOTES

Great served with fruit bread fingers and slivered almonds over the top!

RICE PAPER ROLLS WITH ASIAN DIPPING SAUCE

Serves: makes a total of 10 small or
5 large rolls

Suggested Sides: steamed vegetables,
baked sweet potato

INGREDIENTS

Rice paper sheets (either
10 small or 5 large)

1 small head romaine/
cos lettuce, thinly sliced

1 small Lebanese
cucumber, sliced into
small sticks

1 medium carrot, grated
or sliced into strips

1 small packet tempeh or
tofu, pre-cooked and cut
into thin slices

1 handful cilantro/
coriander, roughly
chopped

Dipping Sauce

2 tsp tamari/soy sauce

2 tsp rice wine vinegar

1 tbsp sweet chilli sauce

 RECIPE NOTES

You can use any fillings that
you like, you could also use
shredded cabbage, bean
sprouts, avocado, thinly
sliced red bell peppers etc

INSTRUCTIONS

1. Run a tea towel under water and wring it out. Fold in half and place on a bench or chopping board. Use this to roll your rice paper rolls on without sticking.

2. Get a large bowl, plate or quiche dish and fill with some lukewarm water. This needs to be large enough to dip the rice paper into.

3. Take a rice paper sheet and drag it through the lukewarm water for a couple of seconds. It will still feel firm but it will continue to soften as you fill it.

4. Place the rice paper flat on the damp tea towel and place some lettuce into the top third of the rice paper. Add cucumber sticks, carrot, tempeh and cilantro. Do not overfill. Fold top edge down, fold side edge in and roll up.

5. Set aside on a plate or non-stick parchment paper until ready to eat. You can also store these in the fridge to eat later or the next day (will keep well for about 3 days).

6. For the dipping sauce, combine all ingredients in a small bowl and stir together until well combined.

7. Dip your spring rolls in the sauce and enjoy!

EGGLESS SALAD SANDWICH

Serves: 2-4

Suggested Sides: steamed vegetables

INGREDIENTS

4 slices of bread (or more if using less mixture)

Base "Egg" Mixture

250g/9oz firm tofu - crumble half of it and roughly chop the other half

½ tsp turmeric powder

½ tsp onion powder

½ tsp garlic powder

⅛ cup water

Dressing

100g/3.5oz (about quarter of a can) canned butter beans/lima beans or cannellini beans including brine

1 tsp dijon mustard

1 small garlic clove

½ tsp lemon juice

½ tsp black salt (kala namak)

1 scallion chopped into small pieces

A few grinds of black pepper

INSTRUCTIONS

1 Firstly, take your block of tofu, crumble half and chop the other half and add into a non-stick frying pan (do not heat yet). Add all the remaining base ingredients except the water and mix well.

2 Put the frypan on a medium to high heat and heat the ingredients for 1-2 minutes until the tofu starts to stick to the pan. Add approximately 1/4 cup water to the pan to soften the tofu and to stop it from sticking. Cook for a minute more and remove from heat.

3 Place the cooked base "egg" mixture into a mixing bowl and set aside.

4 Put all the dressing ingredients except the scallions into a blender and blend till smooth and creamy.

5 Pour the mixture over the base mixture in your bowl and mix through.

6 Add scallions and pepper to suit your taste and mix through the salad.

7 Spread onto sandwiches and serve with your favorite sides!

 RECIPE NOTES

You could add lettuce, tomato, curry powder or anything else that you like to your sandwiches.

SAMOSA TOASTIES

Serves: 1 without sides | 2 with sides

Suggested Sides: crispy salad

INGREDIENTS

4 slices bread

Samosa mix:
1 small potato (½ cup small cubed potato)
½ cup frozen peas
1 tbsp vegetable stock or water
½ tsp garam masala
¼ tsp curry powder
1 tsp onion flakes
1 tsp black mustard seeds
½ tsp cumin seeds
⅛ tsp turmeric powder
Dash white pepper
Salt, optional to taste

INSTRUCTIONS

1 Put potatoes in a non-stick frypan on medium-high heat.

2 Add in spices and stir 5 minutes till potatoes are soft.

3 Add splashes of water as needed to stop the mixture from sticking and to cook through.

4 You want to end up with a dry mixture so it can be used as a filling.

5 Place the mixtures evenly on two slices of bread that have been laid in your sandwich press. Put the top slices of bread on and press shut.

6 Turn sandwich press on and cook till bread is golden brown. Enjoy!

RECIPE NOTES

Great with chilli sauce or chutney on the side.

MEXICAN SALAD BOWL

Serves: 1 without sides | 2 with sides

Suggested Sides: crispy salad

INGREDIENTS

1 large handful of salad greens (pre-packed and washed from supermarket)

1 large handful of coleslaw mix (pre-cut from supermarket)

1 can drained red kidney beans or black beans

½ avocado

¼ cup salsa

1 tbsp chilli sauce (sweet or hot depending on how you like it)

1 small handful of oil free corn chips (or baked sweet potato!)

INSTRUCTIONS

1 Layer everything in a flat bowl and enjoy!

ITALIAN STYLE BEAN & LENTIL PASTA SALAD

Serves: 2 without sides | 4 with sides

Suggested Sides: crusty bread, steamed vegetables, crispy salad

INGREDIENTS

2 cups cooked pasta

½ large carrot, grated

400g/14oz can kidney beans, drained (or beans of choice)

400g/14oz can brown lentils, drained

1 cup passata (or your favorite Italian tomato based cooking sauce)

1 large handful chopped fresh parsley

1 tbsp dried chives

1 tbsp dijon mustard

2 tsp soy sauce

Chilli flakes, optional and to taste

Salt and pepper to taste

INSTRUCTIONS

1 Place everything into a large bowl, stir through and serve!

CREAMY HERBED GNOCCHI SALAD

Serves: 2 without sides | 4 with sides

Suggested Sides: crusty bread, steamed vegetables, baked tofu, avocado

INGREDIENTS

250g/9oz gnocchi, cooked per packet instructions

1 bunch cilantro, chopped (or basil)

400g/14oz can chickpeas (½ in salad and ½ in dressing)

1 cup cucumber, chopped

Dressing

½ of the chickpeas from above

½ cup plant milk

2 tbsp nutritional yeast flakes

½ tsp dijon mustard

1 clove garlic

1 tbsp lemon juice

½ tsp coarse celtic sea salt

⅛ tsp black pepper

INSTRUCTIONS

1 Place all of the main ingredients in a large bowl.

2 Using a blender, blend the dressing ingredients till smooth and creamy.

3 Pour the dressing into the bowl and mix gently to combine everything well.

SWEET COCONUT RICE SALAD

Serves: 2

Suggested Sides: pears, banana, berries

INGREDIENTS

2 cups cooked basmati rice (I prefer cold from fridge)

⅓ cup dried, flaked or desiccated coconut

⅓ cup pumpkin seeds

1 cup canned pineapple pieces, drained (reserve juice)

1 tbsp chopped fresh mint leaves

Dressing

⅛ cup pineapple juice

2 tbsp coconut cream

1 tbsp lime juice

1 tbsp maple syrup

Optional Toppings:

Lime zest and grated crystalized ginger

INSTRUCTIONS

1 Place all main ingredients in a bowl.

2 Combine all dressing ingredients and pour over the rice salad.

3 Mix through gently to combine and add any extra toppings that you like.

RED RICE SALAD WITH CREAMY POMEGRANATE DRESSING

Serves: 2 without sides | 4 with sides

Suggested Sides: baked tofu, steamed vegetables, baked sweet potatoes

INGREDIENTS

2 cups cooked rice
(I used cold from fridge)
1 grated small beetroot
1 grated carrot
1 tsp cumin seeds

Dressing:
1 tbsp pomegranate molasses
1 tbsp tahini
1 tbsp maple syrup
1 - 2 tbsp water

INSTRUCTIONS

1 Mix all dressing ingredients in a jar with a screw top lid or whisk together in a bowl.

2 Combine dressing with main ingredients and stir through to combine.

 RECIPE NOTES

Serve in banana peppers and sprinkle with paprika and almond flakes. Great with baked tofu or lentils.

SWEET POTATO CABBAGE WRAPS WITH SMOKEY PEANUT DIPPING SAUCE

Serves: 1 without sides | 2 with sides

Suggested Sides: crusty bread

INGREDIENTS

1 - 2 large pita bread

Filling

⅓ large sweet potato, diced into small fingertip sized pieces

1 onion, diced

Salt and pepper to taste

A few cups of water as needed to cook over high heat in a pan until soft.

Fresh: 1 cup red cabbage, shredded

Sauce

1 tbsp smokey BBQ sauce

1 tbsp peanut butter

1 tbsp hot water

INSTRUCTIONS

1   Cook the filling ingredients in a non-stick frypan over medium to high heat until the sweet potato is soft and cooked to your liking.

2   In the meantime mix all of the sauce ingredients together and set aside.

3   Place filling and fresh cabbage onto the pitas and serve with the sauce on the side.

 RECIPE NOTES

Mashed chickpeas and avocado is also a great filling. You could use a cabbage leaf or lettuce leaf instead of a bread wrap to put everything in!

TOFU RICE NOODLE SALAD

Serves: 1 without sides | 2 with sides

Suggested Sides: avocado, steamed vegetables, baked sweet potato

INGREDIENTS

70g/2.5oz firm tofu, sliced lengthways into finger shapes (baked, grilled or air fried till crispy)

200g/7oz wok ready rice noodles, heated in boiled water for about 5 minutes to warm and soften

1 handful fresh chopped herbs eg. cilantro or Thai basil

½ cup red cabbage, sliced

¼ cup broccoli, chopped very small (raw or lightly steam if you prefer)

Sauce

½ tbsp soy sauce

1 tbsp sweet chilli sauce

1 tbsp mixed sesame seeds

1 tbsp peanut butter

Optional:

Add flaked almonds over the top for extra crunch

INSTRUCTIONS

1 Stir fry the cabbage and broccoli in a hot non-stick frypan with splashes of water to deglaze the pan as needed.

2 Add the noodles and stir through for another minute of so.

3 Add sauce ingredients and tofu and stir through for another minute or two.

4 Mix through the fresh herbs and serve.

SHREDDED RED CABBAGE SALAD WITH ASIAN DRESSING

Serves: 1 without sides | 2 with sides

Suggested Sides: baked tofu, avocado

INGREDIENTS

2 cups red cabbage, shredded

5 Brussels sprouts, cut very small or shredded

1 tbsp white sesame seeds

1 handful almonds (or sunflower seeds for crunch) * I soaked my almonds in water overnight and then rinsed the next morning

Dressing

½ tbsp tamari or soy sauce

½ tbsp maple syrup

½ tbsp white vinegar

½ tbsp sweet chilli sauce

INSTRUCTIONS

1 Place everything in a bowl and mix through to combine. Serve with your favorite sides or as is. Enjoy!

TOFU PASTA SALAD WITH LEMON HERB DRESSING

Serves: 2

Suggested Sides: crusty bread, steamed vegetables

INGREDIENTS

70g/2.5oz tofu, sliced or cubed (baked, grilled or air fried)

150g/5oz dry pasta, cook per packet instructions and drain

Add-ins:

1 tbsp dried chives

2 tsp dried herbs (I used mixed Italian herbs)

Dressing - Shake in a jar

½ cup chickpea brine

½ tsp chicken stock powder

4 tsp lemon juice

1 tsp onion flakes

Add-ins:

½ avocado, cubed

1 handful chopped fresh herbs - parsley, cilantro, basil

Salt and pepper to taste

Optional:

Add any fresh leafy greens or steamed vegetables of your choice

INSTRUCTIONS

1 Place everything in a bowl and gently toss to mix everything through.

BROCCOLI POTATO SALAD WITH RED WINE VINEGAR CASHEW CREAM

Serves: 2

Suggested Sides: baked tofu, steamed vegetables, avocado

INGREDIENTS

6 small potatoes cut into cubes or wedges (or leftover cooked potatoes)
1 head broccoli, chopped
1 tbsp dried chives
¼ cup olives, sliced

Dressing

2 tbsp red wine vinegar
½ tsp coarse celtic sea salt
1 tbsp maple syrup
2 tbsp cashews

INSTRUCTIONS

1. Boil potatoes until just tender. Rinse with cold water.

2. Steam broccoli in a steamer above the potatoes or in a separate steamer if you don't have one that stacks above. Rinse with cold water.

3. Blend all dressing ingredients in a small blender until smooth and creamy.

4. Place everything into a salad bowl and give it a gentle stir through to combine everything well.

Hot Out Of The Oven

Black Bean Tacos p.90

"Cheesy" Mediterranean Style Pasta Bake p.84

Sticky Cauliflower Wings p.87

SATAY RICE NOODLES

Serves: 1 without sides | 2 with sides

Suggested Sides: steamed vegetables, baked sweet potato, avocado

INGREDIENTS

200g/7oz thin wok ready rice noodles

150g/5oz tofu, small cubes

100g/3.5oz sliced mushrooms

1 large handful baby spinach

Sauce

1 tbsp soy sauce

1 tbsp sweet chilli

1 tbsp peanut butter

2 tbsp hot boiled water from kettle

INSTRUCTIONS

1 Place all main ingredients in an oven proof dish.

2 Mix the sauce ingredients together in a jar or whisk in bowl and pour over the main ingredients.

3 Mix through and bake 10-12 minutes in a pre-heated 200C/400F oven.

 RECIPE NOTES

If you want slightly crisped noodles cook in a dish without a lid.

OVEN BAKED VEGETABLE POCKETS AND CORN

Serves: 1 without sides | 2 with sides

Suggested Sides: rice, avocado, baked tofu

INGREDIENTS

1 corn cob, cut into 4 pieces
2 cups sliced mushrooms
1 small zucchini, grated

Thickener

½ tsp stock powder
⅛ tsp cornstarch
¼ cup water
1 tsp onion flakes

 **RECIPE NOTES**

Squeeze wedge of lemon into the pocket and leave skin and pulp in there to infuse extra flavor. Coat the corn in chickpea brine, minced garlic and herbs if you have time.

INSTRUCTIONS

1 Preheat your oven on maximum heat.

2 Place the mushrooms and zucchini into a roughly folded parchment paper pocket.

3 Mix the thickening ingredients in a small jar or whisk in a small bowl. Pour over the mushrooms and zucchini and lightly close pocket.

4 Place the pocket into a baking dish and place the corn cobs around it.

5 Bake 10-12 minutes.

10 MINUTE PIZZA

Serves: 1 without sides | 2 with sides

Suggested Sides: potato salad, crispy salad

INGREDIENTS

Pizza

1 whole pita bread (store bought is fine)

¼ cup tomato paste

10 cherry tomatoes, sliced in half

½ cup sliced mushrooms

3 whole falafels (or ¼ cup chickpeas)

1 tsp dried herbs (I used mixed Italian)

1 bunch fresh basil, or any other herb of your choice

Cheesy Sauce (or corn cheese on page 92)

¼ cup nutritional yeast flakes

1 clove garlic

2 tbsp pine nuts

¼ tsp coarse celtic sea salt

⅛ tsp black pepper

2 tbsp tapioca starch

¼-½ cup boiling water (use less for thicker consistency)

INSTRUCTIONS

1 To begin this recipe you will need a pizza tray and a blender.

2 Preheat oven to 200C/400F.

3 Place your pita bread on the pizza tray and evenly cover with tomato paste. Then layer up your toppings.

4 Blend the sauce ingredients in a blender (vent the lid so it doesn't explode from the hot water) and finish the pizza off with a generous splashing of cheesy sauce before placing in the oven for 10-12 minutes.

 RECIPE NOTES

I have shown a basic recipe based on what I had in the fridge. You can do the same. Leftover dips, chutneys and spreads can add a great flavour so take a chance!

CREAMY MUSHROOM PIZZA

Serves: 2 pizzas

Suggested Sides: crispy salad

INGREDIENTS

2 pita bread (round flat bread)

400g/14oz mushrooms, sliced (I used king oyster)

Sauce

Dash white pepper

2 tbsp nutritional yeast flakes

1 tsp coarse celtic sea salt

100ml/3.5oz plant milk

¼ cup vegetable stock

2 tsp tapioca

1 tbsp onion flakes

1 tsp dried Italian herbs

Optional Toppings:

Fresh herbs, corn kernels, sliced olives, avocado

INSTRUCTIONS

1 Preheat oven to 200C/400F.

2 Mix all of the sauce ingredients together in a bowl or screw top jar and set aside.

3 Cook the mushrooms in a medium to hot frypan until softened and most of the liquid is cooked away.

4 Add sauce mixture and stir for a few minutes to thicken.

5 Spread mushroom sauce mixture over two pita breads and bake in oven for about 10 minutes or until cooked to your liking.

6 Once cooked, add any extra toppings that you like. They taste best added fresh over the cooked pizza!!

MIDDLE EASTERN STYLE QUINOA

Serves: 2

Suggested Sides: steamed vegetables, crispy salad, baked sweet potato, baked tofu

INGREDIENTS

½ cup quinoa, pre-cooked (cold from fridge is perfect)

400g/14oz can crushed tomatoes

400g/14oz can 5 bean mix (or beans of choice), drained

1 round slice of eggplant, cut into small cubes

2 tsp paprika

1 tbsp soy sauce

Optional Toppings:
Top with pinenuts, raisins and coriander or parsley.

INSTRUCTIONS

1 Preheat oven to 200C/400F.

2 Mix everything together in an ovenproof dish and bake 12 minutes or until heated and cooked to your liking.

3 Top with optional toppings of your choice and serve!

 RECIPE NOTES

Great with za'atar cream from page 88.

RICE NOODLE BAKE WITH CREAMY WHITE BEAN SAUCE

Serves: 1 without sides | 2 with sides

Suggested Sides: steamed vegetables, avocado, baked tofu, baked sweet potato

INGREDIENTS

62g/2oz pack vermicelli rice noodles (soften in hot boiled and drained)

100g/3.5oz mushrooms, sliced

1 zucchini, sliced into thin disks or small cubes

1 tsp dried Italian herbs

1 tsp dried chives

Dash white pepper

400g/14oz can cannellini beans (use half can and remainder with liquid for sauce)

¼ cup water

Sauce:

½ can of the beans and the can liquid from above

1 tbsp nutritional yeast flakes

¼ tsp coarse celtic sea salt

INSTRUCTIONS

1 Preheat oven to 200C/400F.

2 Blend sauce ingredients in a blender until smooth and creamy.

3 Stir everything together in an ovenproof dish and bake about 10 minutes at 200C.

"CHEESY" MEDITERRANEAN STYLE PASTA BAKE

Serves: 4 without sides | 6 with sides
Suggested Sides: crusty bread,
crispy garden salad

INGREDIENTS

250g/9oz (dry weight) macaroni, cooked (use ½ cup for sauce)

Sauce
2 tbsp tapioca flour
1 cup plant milk
1 tbsp nutritional yeast flakes
2 tsp coarse celtic sea salt
½ cup of the cooked macaroni (from above)

Add-ins:
100g/3.5oz sundried tomato pieces
1 large chargrilled red bell pepper/capsicum, sliced
1 tsp dried Italian herbs
1 tbsp dried chives
1 tbsp dried onion flakes

Optional Topping:
a sprinkling of paprika or nutmeg

INSTRUCTIONS

1. Preheat oven to 220C/440F.

2. Blend the sauce ingredients until smooth and creamy.

3. Mix half of the sauce together with the cooked macaroni and all add-ins.

4. Place mixture in a baking dish and pour remaining sauce over the top.

5. Sprinkle with paprika or nutmeg.

6. Bake in oven for about 10 minutes or until browned to your liking.

CREAMY VEGETABLE BAKE

Serves: 2 without sides | 4 with sides

Suggested Sides: crusty bread, avocado, steamed vegetables, baked sweet potato, baked tofu

INGREDIENTS

½ small eggplant, sliced
1 medium zucchini, sliced
1 small grated potato

Sauce
½ cup cashews
¼ cup nutritional yeast flakes
100g/3.5oz tofu
1 cup plant milk or vegetable stock

Topping
½ cup lightly crushed up Corn Flakes
Sprinkling of paprika or nutmeg

INSTRUCTIONS

1 Preheat oven to 220C/440F.

2 Blend sauce ingredients until smooth and creamy.

3 Combine everything together and top with crushed Corn Flakes (or dry breakfast flakes of choice such as bran flakes or rice bubbles) and sprinkle with paprika.

4 Bake for 10 minutes or till cooked to your liking.

 RECIPE NOTES

This does have a slightly soft texture, add ¼ cup chickpea flour to the sauce for a thicker consistency and to be more quiche like.

SAVORY BAKED FRENCH TOAST

Serves: 2

Suggested Sides: steamed vegetables, avocado, hummus

INGREDIENTS

4 slices sourdough bread (or bread of choice, stale is fine)

Batter

¾ cup besan flour

1 tsp salt

¼ tsp white pepper

⅛ cup nutritional yeast flakes

2 tsp dried chives

¾ cup plant milk

Optional Toppings:
Mushrooms, herbs

INSTRUCTIONS

1   Preheat oven to 220C/440C.

2   Mix batter ingredients in a bowl until well combined and smooth.

3   Coat bread slices in the batter and lay into a baking dish. Use parchment paper if you don't want it to stick.

4   Top with mushrooms, tomato, herbs etc like you would a pizza if you like.

5   Bake for 10 to 12 minutes until set and cooked through to your liking.

 RECIPE NOTES

Great served with avocado and sweet chilli sauce!

STICKY CAULIFLOWER WINGS

Serves: 1 without sides | 2 with sides

Suggested Sides: steamed vegetables, rice, quinoa

INGREDIENTS

1 small head of cauliflower, cut into small florets (lightly pre cooked/steamed or use thawed frozen)

Sauce

1 clove garlic, minced

1 tbsp soy sauce

2 tbsp hoisin sauce

1 tsp maple syrup

1 tbsp sweet chilli sauce

INSTRUCTIONS

1 Preheat oven to maximum heat.

2 Mix everything together until well coated.

3 Bake until crisped to your liking, turn a few times throughout the cooking process to crisp up on all sides.

EGGPLANT POLENTA BITES WITH ZA'ATAR CREAM

Serves: 1 without sides | 2 with sides
Suggested Sides: crusty bread,
steamed vegetables, avocado, baked tofu,
baked sweet potato

INGREDIENTS

8 thin slices eggplant
(about 4mm/1/8 inch
thick)
½ cup chickpea brine
⅛ cup Pan (or chickpea
flour)
½ cup rice bubbles
2 tbsp nutritional yeast
flakes
Salt and pepper to taste

Optional Topping:
Mushroom slices

Za'atar Cream
2 tbsp pinenuts (or
cooked chickpeas)
3 tbsp plant milk
1 tbsp za'atar (or sesame
seeds mixed with sumac)
⅛ tsp coarse celtic sea salt
½ tsp maple syrup

INSTRUCTIONS

1 Preheat oven to 200C/400F.

2 Place eggplant slices onto a pizza
tray lined with non-stick parchment
paper.

3 Mix all of the main ingredients
and spread evenly on top of all the
eggplant slices.

4 Add sliced mushrooms on top if
using.

5 Place in oven for about 10 minutes or
until cooked to your liking.

 RECIPE NOTES

Serve on a bed of spinach (2-4 handfuls)
and drizzle with the za'atar cream.

LENTIL BLACK BEAN "CHEESY" NACHOS

Serves: 2 without sides | 4 with sides
Suggested Sides: steamed vegetables, avocado, crispy salad, baked sweet potato

INGREDIENTS

Base
1 bag oil-free corn chips (or potato wedges are good too)

Stretchy "Cheese"
2 tbsp tapioca flour
1 cup plant milk
1 tbsp nutritional yeast flakes
2 tsp coarse celtic sea salt
⅓ cup cashews (or cannellini beans or chickpeas)

Bean Mix
400g/14oz can brown lentils, drained
1 carrot, grated
¼ tsp smoked paprika
¼ tsp ground cumin
1 tsp soy sauce
Salt and pepper to taste
½ cup black beans, mashed lightly

Layer
1 jar salsa

Optional Toppings
Sliced olives
Avocado
Fresh herbs

INSTRUCTIONS

1 Preheat oven to 200C/400F.

2 Make the cheese sauce by placing the sauce ingredients in a blender and blending until very smooth.

3 Add sauce mixture to a medium hot non-stick pan or pot and stir for a few minutes until thick and stretchy. Remove from heat and set aside.

4 Combine all the bean mix ingredients in a shallow bowl and mash roughly with a fork.

5 Place the corn chips as a base layer in a quiche dish or preferred ovenproof dish of your choice.

6 Place bean mix on top, followed by salsa, then stretchy "cheese".

7 Bake for about 5 minutes and serve hot topped with olives, avocado and fresh herbs!

BLACK BEAN TACOS

Serves: 2 without sides | 4 with sides

Suggested Sides: steamed vegetables, baked sweet potato

INGREDIENTS

4 taco shells

Bean Mix
1 small carrot, grated
½ cup black beans
¼ tsp smoked paprika
½ tsp cumin
1 tsp soy sauce
Dash white pepper
Salt to taste

Optional Extras
Lettuce
Tomato
Avocado
Fresh herbs
Salsa
Sweet chilli sauce
Cashew sour cream
Lemon or lime wedges

INSTRUCTIONS

1   Preheat oven to 180C/360F.

2   Place taco shells on a baking tray and set aside.

3   Combine all the bean mix ingredients in a shallow ovenproof bowl and mash roughly with a fork.

4   Place taco shells and bean mixture in the oven and bake for about 7 minutes until taco shells are warm and crispy.

5   Place bean mixture evenly into the taco shells and add any extras that you like.

6   Serve immediately while shells are still hot.

CRUMBED CHICKPEA PATTIES

Serves: 2 without sides | 4 with sides

Suggested Sides: steamed vegetables, rice, baked sweet potato

INGREDIENTS

400g/14oz can chickpeas, drained (reserve liquid)
1 tbsp dijon mustard
½ cup rice bubbles
1 tsp ground cumin

Coating
½ cup flour (or Pan corn flour)
Dash white pepper
3 tsp dried chives
1 tsp vegetable stock powder

INSTRUCTIONS

1 Preheat oven to 220C/440F.

2 Line a pizza tray with some non-stick parchment paper.

3 Mix the main ingredients together until well combined and then shape them into 4 flat patties.

4 Mix all of the coating ingredients in a shallow bowl or on a plate.

5 Dip the patties into the chickpea brine, followed by the coating mixture.

6 Continue until all 4 patties are done and place them on the tray.

7 Bake for about 10 minutes or until cooked to your liking.

BAKED POTATO WITH BROCCOLI AND CORN "CHEESE"

Serves: 1 without sides | 2 with sides

Suggested Sides: steamed vegetables, crispy salad, baked tofu

INGREDIENTS

4 large or 8 small pre-cooked potatoes

4-8 pieces broccoli, pre-steamed or thawed from frozen

Plus a few corn kernels from the sauce ingredients list below

Corn "Cheese" Sauce

½ cup corn kernels (I used canned)

1 tbsp nutritional yeast flakes

Dash white pepper

1 cup water, vegetable stock or plant milk

2 tbsp tapioca

½ tsp coarse celtic sea salt

INSTRUCTIONS

1 Preheat oven to 200C/400F.

2 Squish the potatoes with palm of your hand to flatten.

3 Put non-stick parchment paper on a pizza tray.

4 Put the potatoes on the tray and straight into the oven to start getting them hot.

5 In the meantime, blend all of the sauce ingredient until smooth and pour the mixture into a medium hot non-stick pan or pot. Stir for a few minutes until the mixture is thick and gooey like melted cheese.

6 Take the potatoes from the oven and place the broccoli on top of the potatoes, put a few of the corn kernels on and top with the corn "cheese".

7 Put back in oven and bake for about 5 minutes until the top is gooey, slightly browned and hot.

HASSELBACK POTATOES WITH AVOCADO AIOLI

Serves: 2 without sides | 4 with sides

Suggested Sides: steamed vegetables, crispy salad, baked tofu

INGREDIENTS

4 large or 8 small potatoes (precooked)

Avocado Aeoli
Half large avocado
1 tbsp lemon juice
1 clove garlic
2 tbsp pinenuts
½ tsp coarse celtic sea salt

Topping
400g can baked beans

INSTRUCTIONS

1 Preheat oven to 200C/400F.

2 Slice the potatoes ¾ way through in hasselback potato style. Pinch sides a bit to open them up and sprinkle with salt and pepper, optional.

3 Put onto a pizza tray lined with non-stick parchment paper and place straight in the oven.

4 If you want hot baked beans for your topping, place them in a small oven proof bowl and put them in the oven with the potatoes.

5 In the meantime, blend or mash all of the avocado aioli ingredients and add a splash of plant milk or vegetable stock if you need a little bit of extra liquid to get the mixture combined into a smooth creamy consistency.

6 Remove the potatoes (and beans) from the oven and top with the beans and avocado aioli.

PINEAPPLE GRILLED "CHEESE" SANDWICHES

Serves: 1-2

Suggested Sides: salad, baked tofu

INGREDIENTS

2 slices bread
2 slices pineapple
(canned and drained)

Corn "Cheese" Sauce

½ cup corn kernels
(I used canned)
1 tbsp nutritional yeast
flakes
Dash white pepper
1 cup water, vegetable
stock or plant milk
2 tbsp tapioca
½ tsp coarse celtic sea salt

INSTRUCTIONS

1   Preheat broiler (grill element in oven).

2   In the meantime, blend all of the sauce ingredient until smooth and pour the mixture into a medium hot non-stick pan or pot. Stir for a few minutes until the mixture is thick and gooey like melted cheese. Set aside.

3   Place pineapple on top of bread and onto a pizza tray.

4   Spread "cheese" across the pineapple and broil/grill for 7-12 minutes until hot and gooey. Fast and tasty!

GRILLED "FRIED" RICE

Serves: 2 without sides | 4 with sides

Suggested Sides: steamed vegetables, baked sweet potato, baked tofu, avocado

INGREDIENTS

2 cups pre-cooked rice

500g/17.5oz stir fried vegetables (pre-steamed or thawed frozen)

150g/5oz diced baked tofu, seitan or black beans

Sauce

1 tbsp soy sauce

1 tbsp sweet chilli sauce

2 tbsp hoisin sauce or teriyaki sauce

INSTRUCTIONS

1 Run rice and vegetables under hot water and place all ingredients in an oven proof dish.

2 Mix together to combine and broil/grill or bake for 10-12 minutes.

3 Salt and pepper to taste.

 RECIPE NOTES

Broiling/grilling will be faster and give a few crispy bits.

BROILED VEGETABLE SKEWERS

Serves: 1 without sides | 2 with sides
(Makes 6 skewers total)

Suggested Sides: rice, steamed vegetables, crispy salad, bread, baked sweet potato

INGREDIENTS

200g/7oz firm tofu
1 small red bell pepper, cut into small squares
½ onion
1 medium zucchini, sliced into thick discs

Sauce/Marinade
1 tbsp BBQ sauce
1 tbsp soy sauce
1 tsp maple syrup
¼ tsp sriracha
5 to 10 grind black pepper

INSTRUCTIONS

1 Thread all of the main ingredients onto skewers.

2 Place onto a baking tray lined with non-stick parchment paper.

3 Mix all of the sauce ingredients and pour half of the sauce on the skewers. Turn them over and pour on the rest.

4 Broil/grill for 3-4 minutes on each side.

5 Remove and serve with your favorite side. I like them with rice!

RECIPE NOTES

Use metal skewers, they heat up faster and will cook your food from the inside! Also, add pineapple chunks for a sweet highlight!

CRISPY POTATO & CHICKPEA HASH WITH CREAMED SPINACH DIP

Serves: 1 without sides | 2 with sides

Suggested Sides: crusty bread, steamed vegetables, baked tofu, avocado

INGREDIENTS

2 large cooked potatoes (I used boiled, cubed small and fridge stored)

400g/14oz can chickpeas, drained (reserve brine)

Creamed Spinach

½ packet thawed spinach (125g/4.5oz)

¼ cup cashews

¼ tsp coarse celtic sea salt

Dash white pepper

½ tbsp lemon juice

1 tbsp water

1 tsp dried chives

⅛ cup plant milk

INSTRUCTIONS

1 Preheat oven to maximum heat or turn on your broiler (grill element in your oven).

2 Line a baking tray with non-stick parchment paper.

3 Spread chickpeas and potatoes evenly on your tray and add enough brine to coat as you would if using oil. Season to taste and bake in oven until crisped to your liking. Broil/grill for faster crispier finish.

4 In the meantime, blend the creamed spinach ingredients in a small blender.

5 Serve everything together. YUM!

Slow Cooker Meals

Slow Cooked Shredded Jackfruit p.102

Gluten Free "Chorizo" with Jacket Potatoes p.115

Crumbled Tofu Bourguignon p.111

CHUNKY VEGETABLE PASTA POT

Serves: 2 without sides | 4 with sides

Suggested Sides: crusty bread, steamed vegetables, baked sweet potato

INGREDIENTS

225g/8oz dry pasta
400g/14oz can diced tomatoes
400g/14oz can 5 bean mix, or any beans of your choice
1 zucchini, chopped or sliced
1 cup eggplant, diced
1 large onion, diced
1 tbsp dried Italian herbs
1 tsp coarse celtic sea salt
2 cups water

Blend:

½ cup cashews
¼ cup nutritional yeast flakes
100g/3.5oz tofu
1 cup plant milk or vegetable stock
1 tsp stock powder or salt to taste

INSTRUCTIONS

1 Blend the sauce mixture until smooth and creamy.

2 Place everything into your slow cooker and cook on low for 3 hours.

 RECIPE NOTES

Top with fresh lemon wedge, avocado and freshly chopped parsley.

POTATO AND BEAN HOT POT

Serves: 2 without sides | 4 with sides

Suggested Sides: crusty bread, steamed vegetables, rice

INGREDIENTS

4 small potatoes, cubed

425g/15oz can baked beans in tomato sauce

½ cup water or vegetable stock

200g/7oz mushrooms, sliced

2 handfuls baby spinach leaves

1 large handful fresh chopped herbs, I use cilantro

1 tsp dried onion flakes

1 tsp paprika

INSTRUCTIONS

1 Place everything into your slow cooker, stir through to combine and cook on low for 3-4 hours.

SLOW COOKED SHREDDED JACKFRUIT

Serves: 2 without sides | 4 with sides

Suggested Sides: steamed vegetables, rice, quinoa, avocado, baked sweet potato

INGREDIENTS

1-2 cans jackfruit, rinsed and cores removed, chopped into chunks

1 tsp coarse celtic sea salt

½ tsp ground black pepper (about 30 to 40 grinds)

1 bell pepper/capsicum, thinly sliced

1 medium onion, halved and sliced lengthways

6 cloves garlic, minced

1 ½ cups vegetable stock

400g/14oz can diced tomatoes, including the juices

⅛ cup red wine, optional

1 tsp cumin powder

1 tsp dried oregano

½ cup sliced olives (I used green)

1 tbsp vinegar

1 medium carrot, sliced

½ can black beans (or beans of your choice)

Optional

1 potato, chopped small

INSTRUCTIONS

1 Place everything into your slow cooker, stir through to combine and cook on low for 6 hours.

THAI VEGETABLE CURRY

Serves: 2 without sides | 4 with sides

Suggested Sides: steamed vegetables, rice, quinoa

INGREDIENTS

2 cups coconut cream
¼ cup peanut butter
1 - 2 tbsp red or green curry paste
1 tbsp soy sauce
2 tbsp lemon juice
1 tbsp maple syrup
2 cloves garlic, minced
½ cup vegetable stock
½ tsp ground ginger
⅛ tsp chilli flakes
2 medium courgettes/ zucchinis
200g/½ pound green beans
400g/14oz chickpeas, drained
2 large portobello mushrooms, sliced

INSTRUCTIONS

1 Place everything into your slow cooker, stir through to combine and cook on low for 3-5 hours.

 RECIPE NOTES

Top with lemon wedges, freshly chopped herbs such as coriander and toasted coconut.

MIDDLE EASTERN SPICED EGGPLANT

Serves: 2 without sides | 4 with sides

Suggested Sides: steamed vegetables, fresh green salad, baked tofu

INGREDIENTS

1 large eggplant, cut into wedges

1 cup dry red lentils, rinsed

400g/14oz can crushed tomatoes, including the juices

1 tbsp dried coriander powder

1 tbsp sumac

½ tbsp cumin seeds

1 tsp cinnamon

1 tsp turmeric

2 tsp minced garlic

1 tsp coarse celtic sea salt

500ml/2 cup water

½ cup soy sauce

½ cup dried raisins

½ cup vinegar

INSTRUCTIONS

1 Place everything into your slow cooker, stir through to combine and cook on low for 8 hours.

 RECIPE NOTES

Top with fresh lemon, coriander or parsley and pinenuts.

TOFU BBQ HAMBURGERS WITH LEMON GARLIC POTATOES

Serves: 2 without sides | 4 with sides

Suggested Sides: steamed vegetables, crispy fresh salad, avocado

INGREDIENTS

450g block of firm tofu

Sauce

2 tbsp smokey BBQ sauce

1 tbsp dijon

½ tsp liquid smoke

1 tbsp peanut butter

Lemon Potatoes

2 large potatoes cut into fingers or cubes

2 smashed garlic cloves

2 tsp dried chives

Salt and pepper to taste

2 lemon wedges

 RECIPE NOTES

Serve on hamburger buns with lettuce, tomato, pickles and mustard!

INSTRUCTIONS

1 Line your slow cooker with non stick parchment paper.

2 Prepare your tofu burgers by slicing through the centre lengthways to make 4 pieces. Use a cookie cutter or glass to cut 4 circles (burgers)!

3 Prick tofu circles with a fork all over and on both sides.

4 Mix together the sauce ingredients and spread evenly across all of the tofu burgers.

5 Place them on the parchment paper in your slow cooker and leave room on one side to add the potatoes.

6 For the potatoes get a dinner plate sized piece of parchment paper and lay it on top of a slightly large sized piece of aluminum foil.

7 Place all of the lemon potato ingredients on the parchment paper, squeeze the lemon over the top and put the lemon skin on top of potatoes (discard once cooked).

8 Wrap the potato mixture up securely in the parcel and place to one side of the slow cooker.

9 Put the lid on and cook everything on low for 6-8 hours or high 3 hours.

"CHEESY" KALE AND POTATO PARCELS

Serves: 2

Suggested Sides: steamed vegetables, crispy salad, baked sweet potato

INGREDIENTS

2 cups kale, chopped small

2 large potatoes, cubed or cut into small wedges

1 tbsp dried chives

Sauce

½ cup corn kernels

1 tbsp nutritional yeast flakes

Dash white pepper

¾ cup water

2 tbsp tapioca

½ tsp coarse celtic sea salt

1 clove garlic, minced or sliced

INSTRUCTIONS

1 Mix all of the sauce ingredients together in a jar with a screw top lid or whisk in a small bowl.

2 Place everything into parchment lined aluminium foil, close it tightly and put into your slow cooker.

3 Turn on and cook on high for 3-4 hours or low 8-10 hours.

 RECIPE NOTES

Serve with crispy garden salad and baked tofu!

SMOKEY BBQ CABBAGE ROLLS

Serves: 2

Suggested Sides: steamed vegetables, crispy salad, baked sweet potato

INGREDIENTS

6 large cabbage leaves

Filling
150g firm tofu
1 cup cooked rice
1 tsp dried onion flakes
1 tsp dried Italian herbs
2 tsp dried chives
1 tsp salt, or to taste
¼ cup water (more or less depending on wetness of rice and tofu)

Sauce
¼ cup BBQ sauce (smokey)
½ cup vegetable stock (or ½ cup water + salt or 1 tsp soy sauce)
1 tbsp cornstarch
¼ cup water

INSTRUCTIONS

1 Mix all sauce ingredients in a screw top jar or whisk together in a bowl.

2 Place all ingredients (except the sauce) in a bowl and mash everything together. I like to use my hand for this as it's faster.

3 Top each cabbage leaf with the filling mixture at one end, fold in the sides and roll up tightly.

4 Line the slow cooker with some non-stick parchment paper and place the cabbage rolls on top.

5 Coat the rolls with the sauce and cook on low for 4-6 hours.

 RECIPE NOTES

Use mushroom, zucchini or bell peppers instead of cabbage leaves
Soak leaves in hot water while preparing the filling to soften them a little as this makes it easier to roll them.

TOFU SCRAMBLE FILLED PEPPERS & ZUCCHINI

Serves: 2 without sides | 4 with sides
Suggested Sides: steamed vegetables, baked sweet potato, crispy salad, avocado

INGREDIENTS

2 whole bell peppers
1 large zucchini

Filling
Zucchini scoopings
1 large tomato, diced
200g/7oz firm tofu, mashed or crumbled
½ tsp crushed garlic
1 tbsp dried chives
1 tbsp nutritional yeast flakes
10 grinds black pepper
1 tbsp soy sauce
Salt to taste

INSTRUCTIONS

1   Slice bottom off bell peppers just enough so they stand flat but are still closed. Do not cut bottom open. Clean out the insides.

2   Slice zucchini in half lengthways and scoop out the inside of it leaving a reasonable outer layer so it doesn't collapse when cooking.

3   Line the slow cooker with non-stick parchment paper.

4   Mix all of the filling ingredients together in a bowl.

5   Place filling into the bell peppers and zucchini halves.

6   Put everything into the slow cooker and cook on high for 3-4 hours.

KALE & POTATO LASAGNE

Serves: 4 without sides | 6 with sides

Suggested Sides: crusty bread, steamed vegetables, crispy salad

INGREDIENTS

3 instant lasagne sheets (more if you want to make extra layers)

Greens

2 cups chopped kale leaves

1 handful baby spinach leaves

1 tbsp dried chives

Tomato Layer

800g/28oz jar Italian tomato sauce

White Sauce

400g/14oz can cannellini beans, drained

350g/12oz tofu (I used firm)

1 tbsp onion flakes

1 tbsp nutritional yeast flakes

½ tsp white pepper

1 cup plant milk

Optional Toppings:

a sprinkle of paprika or nutmeg

INSTRUCTIONS

1   Blend all of your white sauce ingredients until smooth. Set aside.

2   Place a thin layer of the tomato sauce on the bottom of your slow cooker.

3   Next, place a lasagne sheet on top.

4   Then add a layer of the white sauce.

5   Keep layering and finish with a layer of the white sauce and sprinkle with paprika or nutmeg.

6   Cook on low for 6 to 8 hours.

SLOW COOKED SEITAN

Serves: 4 - 8 depending on sides

Suggested Sides: steamed vegetables, rice, baked sweet potato, crispy salad

INGREDIENTS

Dry

1½ to 2 cups vital wheat gluten

½ cup tapioca

¼ cup rice bubbles

2 tbsp nutritional yeast flakes

1 tsp cumin powder

1 tbsp dried chives

1 tsp dried onion flakes

⅛ tsp white pepper

Wet

1¼ cup cold water

1 tbsp Massel "beef style" vegetable stock powder

1 tbsp soy sauce

1 cup sliced mushrooms, chopped small

¼ tsp liquid smoke (or 1 tbsp smoked paprika)

2 cloves garlic, minced

Broth

4 cups water or vegetable stock

2 tbsp soy sauce

2 tsp crushed garlic

INSTRUCTIONS

1 Mix all of the dry ingredients together in a bowl.

2 In a separate bowl, combine all the wet ingredients.

3 Pour the wet ingredients into the dry and knead for about 30 seconds.

4 Break into 4 portions and set aside.

5 Place all of the broth ingredients into the slow cooker and add the dough pieces.

6 Cook on low for 10-12 hours.

 RECIPE NOTES

Serve hot with your favorite sides or let cool and keep in fridge or freezer until ready to use.

CRUMBLED TOFU BOURGUIGNON

Serves: 2 without sides

Suggested Sides: steamed vegetables, rice, quinoa, baked sweet potato, mashed potato

INGREDIENTS

225g firm tofu, crumbled
1 tsp liquid smoke
¼ cup red wine, optional
1 cup vegetable stock
¼ cup ketchup or smokey BBQ sauce
2 tbsp soy sauce
2 tbsp cornstarch
2 cloves garlic, sliced
6 small potatoes, halved or quartered
1 tbsp dried Italian herbs
2 medium carrots, sliced
3 large portobello mushrooms, sliced thick
1 tsp coarse celtic sea salt
Freshly ground black pepper to taste (I used about 20 grinds)

INSTRUCTIONS

1 Place everything in your slow cooker, stir through to combine well. Cook on low for 6 hours (will depend on the type of potatoes that you use).

 RECIPE NOTES

Garnish with fresh herbs when serving!

STEAMED VEGETABLES WITH LEMON HERB SAUSAGES

Serves: 2 without sides | 4 with sides

Suggested Sides: hot dog rolls, salad, mustard, avocado, baked sweet potato

INGREDIENTS

Dry

¼ cup tapioca

½ - ¾ cup vital wheat gluten (start with ½ cup and add more if needed)

1 tsp caraway seeds

½ tsp white pepper

½ tsp lemon zest

2 tbsp nutritional yeast flakes

¼ cup Rice Bubbles

Wet

½ cup water

¼ cup lemon juice

½ tsp liquid smoke

1 tsp coarse celtic sea salt

1 large garlic clove

½ cup corn kernels

50g breadcrumbs or stale bread

1 tbsp Italian herbs

1 tbsp dried chives

Vegetables

Any vegetables that you like eg. corn, broccoli, carrots, kale

INSTRUCTIONS

1. Mix all of the dry ingredients together in a bowl.

2. Blend the wet ingredients in a blender and then pour into the bowl with the dry mix.

3. Knead into a dough for about 30 seconds. Divide into 4 and roll into sausage shapes.

4. Wrap each sausage into a parchment paper lined piece of aluminum foil. You want to roll it up in the foil and then twist the ends tightly and fold them over.

5. Add vegetables of your choice into a heat proof bowl.

6. Fill your slow cooker with water so it is about 3cm/ 1 inch high.

7. Stand the bowl in the water. Place the rolled up sausages across the top of the bowl (or put in another bowl next to it) and cook everything on high for 3 hours or low for about 6 hours.

SWEET POTATO AND GREENS SOUP

Serves: 2 without sides | 4 with sides

Suggested Sides: crusty bread, avocado, rice, quinoa

INGREDIENTS

200g/7oz baby spinach leaves

1 bunch coriander or basil (chopped including stalks for extra flavor)

200g/7oz green beans

600g/21oz sweet potato, sliced or diced

400g/14oz can 5 beans mix or beans of choice, including brine from can

2 tbsp dried chives

¼ cup nutritional yeast flakes

5 cloves garlic, minced

1 tbsp fennel seeds

½ cup vinegar (I used white)

½ tsp white pepper

1 tbsp dijon mustard

1 litre/quart water

½ cup soy sauce

INSTRUCTIONS

1 Place everything in slow cooker, stir through to combine everything well and cook on low for 8-10 hours.

BLACK BEAN AND SWEET POTATO STEW

Serves: 2 without sides | 4 with sides

Suggested Sides: steamed vegetables, rice, quinoa

INGREDIENTS

500g/17.5oz (6 small) sweet potatoes, whole small or large ones cut into wedges

440g/15.5oz can black beans with brine (or use vegetable stock +

1 tsp cornstarch as a substitute for the brine)

4 small garlic cloves, peeled

400g/14oz can chopped tomatoes in juice

1 tsp sweet paprika

¼ tsp cinnamon

½ tsp chilli flakes

1 tsp coriander powder

INSTRUCTIONS

1 Add everything to slow cooker and stir through a few times to make sure all ingredients are well combined.

2 Cook on low for 6-8 hours.

GLUTEN FREE "CHORIZO" WITH JACKET POTATOES

Serves: 2 without sides | 4 with sides

Suggested Sides: hot dog rolls, crispy salad, avocado, steamed vegetables

INGREDIENTS

4-6 medium potatoes with skin on (or sweet potatoes)

Sausages

Wet

1 cup baked beans or beans of your choice
½ tsp chilli flakes
1 tsp coarse celtic sea salt
⅛ tsp black pepper
3 tsp paprika
1 tsp caraway seeds
1 clove garlic
½ tsp liquid smoke
⅛ cup soy sauce

Dry Mix

1 tbsp dried chives
3 tsp dried Italian herbs
1 tsp coriander powder
½ cup tapioca flour
½ cup sorghum flour

INSTRUCTIONS

1 Mix all of the dry ingredients together in a bowl.

2 Blend the wet ingredients in a blender and then pour into the bowl with the dry mix.

3 Knead into a dough and divide into 4 portions and roll into sausage shapes.

4 Wrap each sausage into a parchment paper lined piece of aluminum foil. You want to roll it up in the foil and then twist the ends tightly and fold them over.

5 Wrap the potatoes in aluminium foil also and place into a heat proof bowl.

6 Fill your slow cooker with water so it is about 3cm/1 inch high.

7 Stand the bowl in the water. Place the rolled up sausages across the top of the bowl (or put in another bowl next to it) and cook everything on high for 3-4 hours or low for about 6-8 hours.

RED LENTIL AND POTATO DAHL

Serves: 4 without sides | 6 with sides
Suggested Sides: crusty bread, rice, freshly chopped kale, avocado

INGREDIENTS

2 cups dried split red (pink) lentils, rinsed
1 large potato, cubed into thumb sized pieces
1 garlic clove, minced
400g/14oz can crushed tomatoes
6 cups water or vegetable stock
1 tbsp onion flakes
½ tbsp turmeric powder
1 tsp coriander powder
1 tsp cumin powder
1 tsp black mustard seeds
1 tsp cumin seeds
1 tsp coarse celtic sea salt
½ tsp ground ginger
¼ tsp black pepper (I do about 30 grinds)

INSTRUCTIONS

1 Add everything to slow cooker and stir through a few times to make sure all ingredients are well combined.

2 Cook on low for 8-10 hours or 3 to 4 hours on high.

 RECIPE NOTES

Great served with freshly chopped kale and rice. Top with a wedge of lemon and fresh cilantro and avocado!

PEA AND YAM SOUP

Serves: 6-8

Suggested Sides: crusty bread

INGREDIENTS

450g/16oz bag dried split peas, rinsed well

1 onion, diced

1 large sweet potato, cubed into thumb sized pieces

1 stalk celery, chopped

2 tsp coarse celtic sea salt

1 dried bay leaf

¼ cup parsley, finely chopped

10 cups water (preferably hot boiled from the kettle)

1 tbsp dried chives

1 tsp dried onion flakes

2 tbsp soy sauce

1 tsp liquid smoke

5 dashes white pepper

INSTRUCTIONS

1 Add everything to slow cooker and stir through a few times to make sure all ingredients are well combined.

2 Cook on low for 6-8 hours.

HEARTY POTATO AND CORN VEGETABLE STEW

Serves: 4 without sides | 8 with sides

Suggested Sides: crusty bread, avocado, baked tofu

INGREDIENTS

1 large potato, cubed

4 pieces fresh corn on the cob (1 large cob cut into 4)

1 cup dry green split peas, rinsed

1 kg/2 pound bag frozen vegetables (or fresh cut into small pieces)

3 - 4 cups vegetable stock

1 tbsp onion flakes

1 tsp crushed garlic

½ tbsp turmeric powder

1 tsp caraway seeds

1 tsp coarse celtic sea salt

¼ tsp black pepper

1 tbsp dried chives

½ cup nutritional yeast flakes

INSTRUCTIONS

1 Add everything to slow cooker and stir through a few times to make sure all ingredients are well combined.

2 Cook on low for 6-8 hours or high for 3 hours.

CREAMY MUSHROOM GOULASH

Serves: 2 without sides | 4 with sides

Suggested Sides: crusty bread, rice, steamed vegetables, baked tofu, baked sweet potato

INGREDIENTS

500g/1 pound mixed mushrooms (chunky portobello or whole button mushrooms work well)

1 large carrot, sliced

½ tbsp dijon mustard

1 tbsp tomato paste

1 large onion, diced very small or grated

1 red bell pepper, diced or sliced

1 clove garlic, minced

600ml/20floz vegetable stock (I use water + Massel "beef style" vegetable powder)

¼ tsp liquid smoke

1 large potato, cubed small

2 tsp coarse celtic sea salt (less if using salty stock)

½ tsp black pepper (about 30 grinds)

1 tbsp sweet paprika

1 tbsp soy sauce

INSTRUCTIONS

1 Add everything to slow cooker and stir through a few times to make sure all ingredients are well combined.

2 Cook on low for 6-8 hours.

 RECIPE NOTES

If you want the sauce thicker, mix 1 or tbsp of cornstarch with a bit of water and add the slurry mixture to the slow cooker about 1 hour before turning it off. Or mix a few cups full of the mixture in the cooker and blend with ½ cup cashews making sure to vent the lid as the mixture will be hot and you don't want to have the lid blow off from the pressure build up. Add the blended sauce mixture back into the slow cooker and stir through to make it extra thick and creamy.

BUT WAIT! There's more... Join thousands of people just like you who are transforming their health, losing weight, gaining energy and feeling good by eating more plants.

Get my FREE 7 DAY KICKSTART 'SLIM DOWN'
MEAL PLAN
https://cooking-with-plants.teachable.com/p/free-7-
day-kickstart-slim-down-meal-plan

By falling in love with a plant based lifestyle, I reversed my heart-disease and lost over 50 pounds without even trying...

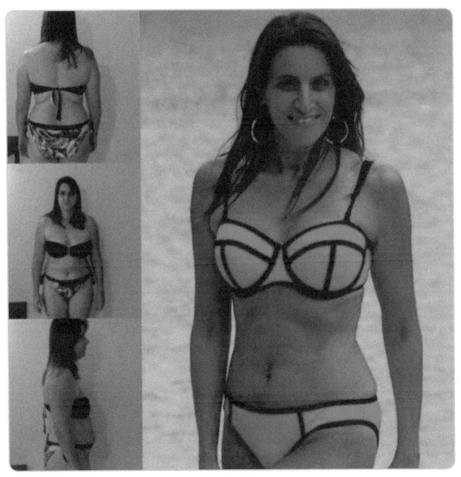

Anja Cass - Cooking With Plants
(Left 183lbs/83kg - Right 130lbs/59kg)

Plant Powered Mastery Course - 21 Day New Body Program!

Everything You Need to Lose Weight, Gain Energy, Sleep Well and Feel Amazing!

WHAT YOU GET:

- A step-by-step guide to ease you into a plant-based lifestyle
- Download a 21 Day Meal Plan (with all recipes)
- Printable Shopping Lists for each week
- Easy-to-use food diary
- Printable Cheat Sheets and Food Lists
- Unlimited access to the online streaming videos, and much more...

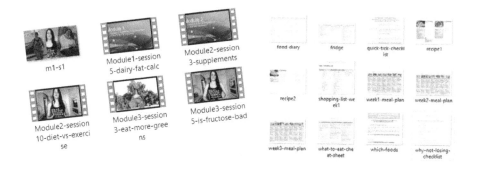

PLUS FREE BONUSSES!

- Invitation only access to the private Plant Powered Mastery Facebook group where you can ask questions and sharte your thoughts in a caring like-minded community setting
- My priority emaill address so you can ask questions at any time

And much more...

WHAT OTHERS ARE SAYING...

Naomi

*" The 3 week meal plan is very practical.
I appreciated that you included leftovers
as part of the planning food for the next day.
We have laminated the meal plans as well as
the food diary journal for easy use.
Thank you."*

– Naomi

Amal

*" I have done a lots of research about nutrition.
I like your plan especially when you do give guidelines
about what are eating every day because sometimes
I just like to put a mean together without
necessarily following a receipe"*

– Amal

Check out my PLANT POWERED MASTERY COURSE -
21 DAY NEW BODY PROGRAM!
https://cooking-with-plants.teachable.com/p/plant-powered-mastery

MORE COOKBOOKS

Since the launch of her debut book, Vegan Made Easy in 2015, Anja has created a range of "must-have" cookbooks that show that anyone can cook nutritious, tasty plant based food regardless of time or ability.

"I've designed my cookbooks the way I always wanted to have a cookbook written for me. With simple instructions and a photo for each recipe so I know what I'm cooking and what it should look like, as well as a user-friendly index so I can find my favorite recipes easily".

CHECK OUT ALL OF THE COOKING WITH PLANTS COOKBOOKS AT:
https://www.cookingwithplants.com

JOIN THE EMAIL ALERTS OF LATEST RECIPES AT:
http://www.cookingwithplants.com

JOIN THE COOKING WITH PLANTS FACEBOOK COMMUNITY
https://www.facebook.com/groups/cookingwithplants/

INSTAGRAM
http://www.instagram.com/cookingwithplants

YOUTUBE
http://bit.ly/CookingWithPlants

PINTEREST
https://www.pinterest.com/cookingplants/vegan-recipes/

I have lost over 50 pounds and reversed heart issues. A plant based lifestyle has totally changed my life and brought back my health, energy and vitality! The journey all started when I watched the movie Forks Over Knives - to get your own copy of this life changing dvd, visit my affiliate page on Amazon if interested at http://amzn.to/1MgHoDy And I also read The China Study: http://amzn.to/1MgHsDt

Printed in Australia
AUHW011002081118
304842AU00003BA/3

9 781925 833201